Walk Aroun

Sturmgeschütz III Ausf. G

By Tom Cockle

Color by Don Greer and Andrew Probert

Illustrated by Mariano Rosales

Armor Walk Around Number 2

squadron/signal publications

Introduction

The *Sturmgeschütz III Ausführung G* (StuG III Ausf. G) was the culmination of assault gun development in the German Army during World War Two. Originally designed in 1937 as an infantry support vehicle, the StuG III was armed with the same 7.5 CM KwK 37 L/24 gun mounted in the **PzKpfw IV Ausf. A**. Krupp was contracted to design the gun, while Daimler-Benz designed the superstructure and chassis. Five vehicles were built on **PzKpfw III Ausf. B** chassis and were reported as being operational in October of 1939. The hulls utilized a soft steel superstructure and were used only for training purposes. The **StuG III Ausf. A** — also built by Daimler-Benz — became the first production series in January of 1940 and was built on the **PzKpfw III Ausf. F** chassis. Subsequently, *Altmärkische Kettenwerk GmbH* (Alkett) was contracted to assemble the **StuG III Ausf. B** instead of Daimler-Benz. After the Ausf. B, only minor improvements to the basic design were made up to the production of the **StuG III Ausf. E**. Firepower was greatly increased with the installation of the new 7.5 cm StuK40 L/43 in the **StuG III Ausf. F** beginning in March of 1942. After the production of 120 vehicles, the gun was changed to the StuK40 L/48, which remained in use throughout production of the StuG III Ausf. G until the end of the war. By early 1943, *Mühlenbau und Industrie AG* (MIAG) was also employed in assembling the StuG III Ausf. G in an effort to increase production rates. *Maschinenfabrik Augsburg-Nürnberg* (MAN) also provided Pzkpfw III tank chassis for conversion to StuG IIIs.

Since the StuG III began to be used more in the anti-tank role, the infantry was left without dedicated fire support. A new vehicle, consisting of the 10.5 cm lFH18 howitzer mounted on a StuG III chassis, was developed and designated **StuH 42** (*Sturmhaubitze 42*). The first five vehicles were completed on StuG III Ausf. F chassis with another four on **StuG III Ausf. F/8** chassis in October of 1942. Delivery of the first production StuH 42, all of which were built by Alkett, began in March of 1943 and continued until the end of the war.

The first StuG III Ausf. Gs were produced in December of 1942 and featured a new superstructure that had several improvements over the previous designs. The crew compartment extended out over the tracks on both sides and had a sloped front. Initially, the slope was steeper, but this was changed in January of 1943, along with relocating the fume extraction ventilator to the rear wall of the crew compartment. One major improvement was the installation of a commander's cupola that could rotate 360° and provide the gun commander with better all around vision. A ball bearing shortage led to the cupola being fixed in position in September of 1943, but when ball bearing production increased, this feature was reintroduced in August of 1944.

During its production run, the StuG III Ausf. G incorporated several other improvements. When the slope of the side panniers increased in January of 1943, it was no longer possible to install the driver's side view port. This was replaced with a pistol port plug. Also beginning in December of 1943, a hinged machine gun shield was introduced that provided the gunner with some forward protection. Two brackets welded on the shield's rear face allowed the 7.92MM MG34 or MG42 machine gun to be mounted for use against ground as well as aerial targets. The driver's periscopes were dropped in February of 1943 and the 30MM armor plates bolted around the driver's visor was changed to a single plate to cover the space. Experiments had proven the effectiveness of thin, spaced armor plates called 'Schürzen', and these were ordered to be installed on new StuG III, PzKpfw IV, and Panthers in time for the Kursk offensive in July of 1943. The additional 30MM armor plates first installed on StuG III Ausf. Fs, were replaced by a single 80MM plate on the hull front of the StuG III Ausf. G beginning in May of 1943. The right side of the superstructure was also increased to 80MM in June of 1944. By September of 1943, 'Zimmerit' anti-magnetic mine coating began to be installed at the MIAG plant, followed in December by Alkett, with its distinctive 'waffle' pattern. In October of 1943, a shot deflector was installed in front of the commander's cupola — at first only at the Alkett plant, and then on all StuG III produced after February of 1944. A new cast gun mantlet, called

Acknowledgements and Photo Credits

I would like to thank the following people whose contributions made this book possible: my good friend Gary Edmundson who provided me with copies of photographs from both the Patton Armor Museum at Fort Knox, Kentucky and the Ordnance Museum of the Aberdeen Proving Ground, Maryland; Robert Decker for his photographs of the StuG III at the Patton Armor Museum; Ron Volstad for the photographs of the StuG III in Jacques Littlefield's collection and for twenty years of friendship, inspiration, and support in my hobby; Jim Carswell and Jarmo Lindgren for their photographs from the Finnish Armor Museum (*Panssarimuseo*), Parola, Finland; Frederic Erk for his valuable assistance in obtaining photographs at the *Musee des Blindés* at Saumur, France and Colonel Olmer, Director of the Museum for permission to use the photographs; and my daughter Jaime, who took time out from her European odyssey to travel to the *Panzermuseum* in Thun, Switzerland especially to take photographs for me. The remaining photographs are of a StuG III Ausf. G formerly at Sarcee Barracks in Calgary, Alberta, Canada.

ISBN 0-89747-434-1

If you have any photographs of aircraft, armor, soldiers or ships of any nation, particularly wartime snapshots, why not share them with us and help make Squadron/Signal's books all the more interesting and complete in the future. Any photograph sent to us will be copied and the original returned. The donor will be fully credited for any photos used. Please send them to:

Squadron/Signal Publications, Inc.
1115 Crowley Drive
Carrollton, TX 75011-5010

Если у вас есть фотографии самолётов, вооружения, солдат или кораблей любой страны, особенно, снимки времён войны, поделитесь с нами и помогите сделать новые книги издательства Эскадрон/Сигнал ещё интереснее. Мы переснимем ваши фотографии и вернём оригиналы. Имена приславших снимки будут сопровождать все опубликованные фотографии. Пожалуйста, присылайте фотографии по адресу:

Squadron/Signal Publications, Inc.
1115 Crowley Drive
Carrollton, TX 75011-5010

軍用機、装甲車両、兵士、軍艦などの写真を所持しておられる方はいらっしゃいませんか？どの国のものでも結構です。作戦中に撮影されたものが特に良いのです。Squadron/Signal社の出版する刊行物において、このような写真は内容を一層充実し、興味深くすることができます。当方にお送り頂いた写真は、複写の後お返しいたします。出版物中に写真を使用した場合は、必ず提供者のお名前を明記させて頂きます。お写真は下記にご送付ください。

Squadron/Signal Publications, Inc.
1115 Crowley Drive
Carrollton, TX 75011-5010

(Front Cover) A late StuG III Ausf. G of StuG Brigade 280 parks in the streets of Oosterbeek, Holland in September 1944 during Operation MARKET-GARDEN. It features a waffle pattern *Zimmerit* coating and the *Topfblende* cast mantlet. The vehicles of this unit made extensive use of cut foliage to augment their camouflage during the battle.

(Previous Page) This late StuG III Ausf. G is preserved in Thun, Switzerland and incorporates many of the features of a middle or later production Ausf. G. It is equipped with the solid 80MM armor plate on the right side of the fighting compartment (introduced in May of 1943), the cupola shot deflector (October), and one of the three patterns of steel return rollers that replaced the rubber tired return rollers in December of 1943. A coaxial machine gun was installed in the welded gun mantlets in June of 1944 — evident by the hole in the upper right corner.

(Back Cover) This StuH 42 Ausf. G, east of Berlin in the spring of 1945, is from the final production run on which muzzle brakes were no longer mounted. The *Schürzen* have been heavily modified to make them less likely to be lost while moving through dense brush.

The *Sturmgeschütz* III was initially designed to provide troops with close-in fire support. The StuG III Ausf. A through E used a modified PzKpfw III tank chassis, a fixed fighting compartment, and a short-barreled, 7.5 CM howitzer. Apart from detail differences, mostly to speed up manufacturing or improve ballistic protection, the vehicles remained externally similar.

the *'Topfblende'*, or 'pot mantlet,' was introduced in November of 1943, although the welded mantlet continued to be produced until the end of the war. Additionally, new steel return rollers made their appearance. Sometime after the beginning of April of 1944, a remotely controlled machine gun mount was installed on the roof. This addition required a change to side opening hatches for the loader/radio operator. A *'Nahverteidigungswaffe'* close in defense weapon first appeared on StuG III in May of 1944. A shortage of this weapon resulted in several StuG IIIs having the hole in the roof simply plated over until October of 1944, when sufficient quantities were available to equip all new vehicles. In June of 1944, a coaxial machine gun was mounted in the welded gun mantlet and later, in October, in the cast gun mantlet.

A total of 7893 StuG III Ausf. Gs were built from December of 1942 until March of 1945. An additional 1211 StuH 42 were completed from October of 1942 until February of 1945.

The StuG III Ausf. G first appeared in its final form in December of 1942. The major change over its predecessors was a new, wider fighting compartment that was fitted with a commander's cupola, providing all around vision. On the initial production vehicles, the front sloping plate on the pannier extending over the tracks was steeper and the fume extraction ventilator was still mounted centrally on the rear of the fighting compartment roof. The welded box shaped mantlet was originally introduced on the StuG III Ausf. F and F/8.

The StuG III Ausf. F, introduced in early 1942, was the first of the long gun variants and incorporated a 7.5 CM StuK 40 L/43 gun designed to improve performance against enemy tanks. A sub-variant of the Ausf. F, designated Ausf. F/8, was equipped with the improved 7.5 CM StuK 40 L/48 gun and other improvements. The use of the in-production, but obsolescent PzKpfw III chassis, fixed fighting compartment, and powerful gun provided the German Army with a tank hunter that was both inexpensive and easy to produce compared to a turreted tank.

The 50MM (1.97 inch) front plates on the fighting compartment were augmented by 30MM (1.18 inch) plates bolted to their front. The bolt-on plate on the right side was dropped when the main plate was increased from 50MM to 80MM (3.15 inches) in June of 1944. The 30MM armor plates continued to be bolted to the driver's front plate until the end of the war.

The hull side plates were extended and drilled out to create towing brackets beginning with StuG III Ausf. F/8 production and carrying on through Ausf. G production. Steel return rollers were also installed on some vehicles beginning in November of 1943, although rubber tired return rollers continued to be installed until the end of 1944. The spare tracks mounted on the side of the hull helped augment the armor protection of the thin, 30MM hull plates.

Early production StuG III Ausf. Gs were provided with bolt-on 30MM armor plates on the glacis plates — an effort to improve ballistic protection that was applied to several German tank designs. This is an example of an early production vehicle, manufactured in early 1943 and supplied to Finland, with the additional 30MM armor plates bolted to the hull front. The front mudguards were also fixed on the StuG III Ausf. G. Fifty-nine StuG III Ausf. Gs were given to the Finnish Army to support them in their fight against the Russians.

Some StuG III Ausf. F/8s, and the initial production StuG III Ausf. Gs, had additional 30MM armor plates bolted to the two 50MM hull front plates. The front plates were ordered increased to 80MM in February of 1943. The first vehicles with the new 80MM plates were produced in May of 1943.

The StuG III Ausf. F/8 and G engine decks were the same as that introduced on the PzKpfw III Ausf. J. The 50MM rear plate is supported by four braces to the rear hull plate and secured by welding and four rows of conical shaped bolts. The Ausf. G rear mudguard was fixed in position. The mudguard was hinged on earlier variants.

4

Early production Ausf. Gs soon had the ventilator fan moved from the roof to the rear plate in an effort to increase space in the fighting compartment. The fan opening was covered by a circular armor plate. The additional bolt-on armor plate and spare track brackets mounted on the hull sides are not an original component; these were added by the Finnish Army.

This late production *Sturmhaubitze* (StuH) 42 Ausf. G incorporates many features of a late production vehicle. The single 80MM plate on the front right side of the superstructure was installed on vehicles produced beginning in June of 1944. The mount for the remote controlled MG34, first installed in April of 1944, is built into the roof of the fighting compartment. This vehicle is also equipped with a coaxial MG mount that was first installed in the welded mantlet in June of 1944. The coaxial machine gun was not installed in the cast gun mantlet until after October of 1944. The 10.5 CM howitzer's muzzle brake was discontinued in September of 1944.

The cast *Topfblende* (pot mantlet) was introduced on the StuG III Ausf. G production line in November of 1943. This vehicle is also fitted with one of the three styles of steel return rollers that were also introduced in November. The triangular plate and brackets bolted to the mudguard and superstructure side supported *Schürzen* (skirts) spaced armor plates.

There was a covered opening in the rear plate to insert the inertial crank starter for the vehicle's 265 HP Maybach HL 120 TRM V-12 gasoline engine. The armored cover plate is missing, but the remains of the mounting brackets are still welded to the rear plate. The crank starter was stowed on the rear plate on some StuG III Ausf. G.

The initial production StuG III Ausf. Gs had a steeper side pannier and retained the driver's side vision port. Later in the production run, the angle of the pannier's front plate was changed to improve protection and the side vision port was eliminated. This vehicle is also fitted with the wider *Winterketten* tracks and 30MM bolted armor plates on the lower hull.

The Ausf. G suspension consisted of six torsion bars and trailing arms on each side of the vehicle. The engine has been removed from this StuG III Ausf. G and, over time, the nose heavy vehicle has caused the torsion bars to collapse, lowering the front end.

The driver's side vision port was welded closed. The Germans began welding the ports closed on several armored vehicle designs as part of a wholesale effort to speed production. The side vision ports were later replaced by a single round pistol port closed off by a removable metal plug.

Early Upper Hull

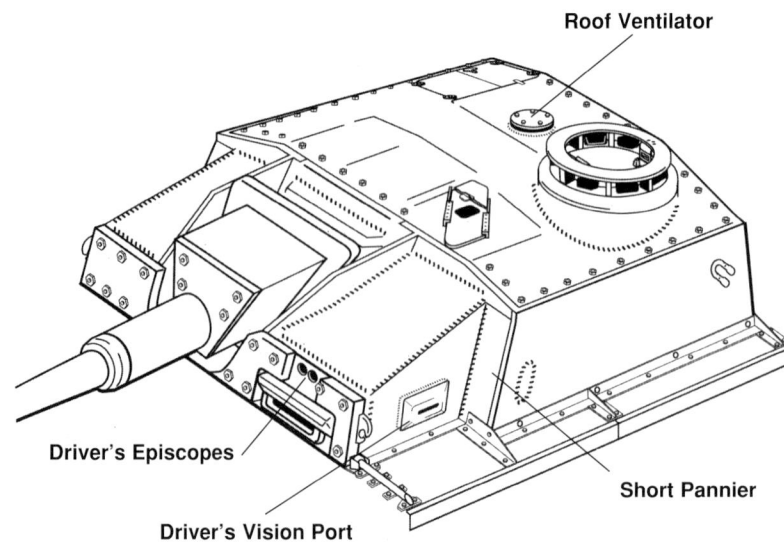

Roof Ventilator

Driver's Episcopes

Driver's Vision Port

Short Pannier

A fully stowed — and then some — StuG III Ausf. G supports German infantry moving across a Russian field. The engine starting crank is stowed on the rear hull plate next to the engine's inertia starting port. The vehicle is equipped with side skirt mounting brackets, but the skirts have long since been lost; the crew has resorted to the use of T-34 tank tracks to augment the hull side armor.

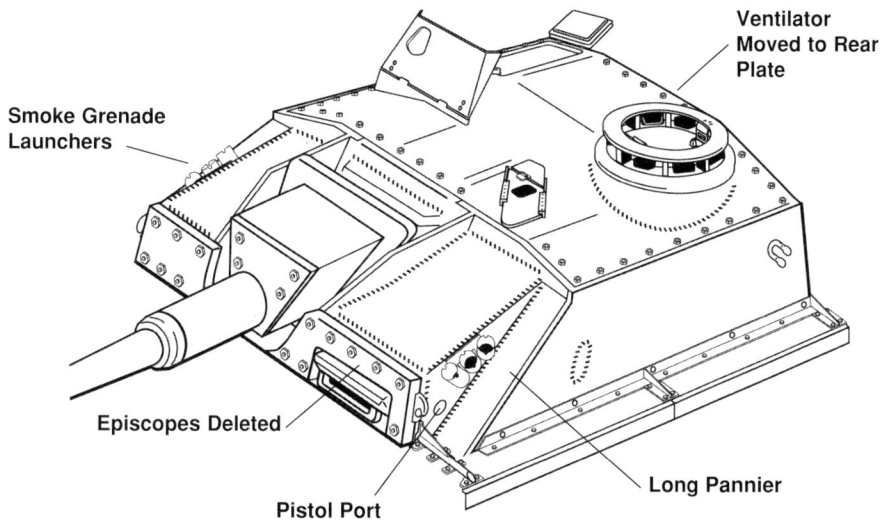

Powerful radiator fans exhausted air through the back of the engine compartment. A sheet metal deflector was installed over the exhaust mufflers to prevent dust from being kicked up by the air flow. The right half of this deflector has been torn away.

The smaller armor plates of the early StuG IIIs employed simple butt joints. The initial production Ausf. Gs continued this practice, but later changed to an interlocking design to improve the weld strength on the larger plates. The interlocking joints in the side of the crew compartment are visible, including the tongue-and-slot joint for the upper side and front plates.

Later Upper Hull

Smoke Grenade Launchers

Ventilator Moved to Rear Plate

Episcopes Deleted

Pistol Port

Long Pannier

(Above) The vehicle engine crank starter was sometimes stowed on the side of the engine's right air intake. The end of the starter crank fitted into the round tube seen on the intake's upper left corner while the handle was held in place by a clamp seen near the front.

(Above Left) Spare track links were frequently mounted on the front hull plate, supported by a steel bar. This provision provided a convenient method of carrying spare track links with the vehicle in case of needed repairs and also provided an additional measure of protection.

(Left) This early production StuG III Ausf. G has the rubber tired return rollers. It also lacks the interlocking weld joints on the corners of the crew compartment side and rear plates and the engine deck plates.

(Above) The loss of the StuG III Ausf. F and Gs as a dedicated infantry support vehicle, resulted in the fitting of a large howitzer to both variants. These vehicles were designated *Sturmhaubitze* (StuH) 42. All StuH 42 Ausf. G were built by Alkett and mounted a 10.5 CM StuH 42 howitzer instead of the 7.5 CM StuK40 gun. The muzzle brake on this example is not original equipment, but is from a 10.5 CM IFH18M field howitzer as used on the Wespe self-propelled gun.

(Above Right) The muzzle brake is missing on this StuH 42 Ausf. G revealing the threaded end of the gun barrel and the rifling inside. The ring on the back of the threads was tightened against the back of the muzzle brake to lock it in place. This vehicle is equipped with the later 80MM (3.15 inch) front hull plates, but retains the earlier 50MM (1.97 inch) upper plates with 30MM (1.18 inch) bolt-on armor.

(Right) The StuH 42 barrel is significantly shorter than that of the 7.5 CM StuK40 and is easily identifiable. Externally, the StuH 42 Ausf. G was identical to the StuG III Ausf. G. Internally, only the breech and ammunition racks were different. This vehicle is equipped with the early rubber tired track return rollers.

(Above Left) The StuG III Ausf. G used a number of various designs of 40 CM (15.75 inch) wide tracks. This track has a different type of cleat with two small dimples on each side, while one link has two notches cut into the cleat. There is also one link that has the open guide tooth configuration.

(Above Center) This set of spare track links displays two types of guide teeth. While both are of the solid type, one track has a small indent on each side of each tooth. Although the various links differed in detail, they remained interchangeable. The tracks were linked together using a single steel pin between each link. A cotter pin was inserted into the pin's end to prevent it from working its way out.

(Above Right) The chevrons cast into the face were designed to provide traction on icy roads. The tracks were manufactured by different firms and several different casting marks are visible. The links also have two different patterns at the ends of the cleats.

(Left) An early production StuG III Ausf. G moves through underbrush somewhere on the Eastern Front. Although the tracks have become impacted with dirt, the cleats remain bright and clean. This vehicle is one of those completed on a PzKpfw III chassis from MAN with welded 30MM plates on the lower hull.

(Above) The StuG III's 40 cm tracks were also used on the PzKpfw III and IV gun tanks. This track type has two flat rectangular notches cut into the cleat. This vehicle is an early production PzKpfw III tank. The track pitch was 120mm (4.7 inches) and there were normally 93 links per side.

(Above Right) The drive sprocket was a complex single piece casting to which the toothed outer ring was bolted. StuG IIIs were often missing the cover cap that protected the nuts fastening the sprocket to the final drive. The cap was a heavy steel stamping.

Tracks

Type:....Single Pin Manganese Steel
Width:...40 cm
Pitch:....12 cm
Links:...93 per side

(Right) Both hull side plates were extended and drilled to provide a towing bracket. A mounting bracket for the spare track link stowage bar is welded to the 80mm front plate just below the tow eye.

11

The drive sprocket was designed to allowed dirt and mud built up inside to be shed through the holes around the outer face. This drive sprocket is equipped with the stamped steel center cap. Casting marks on the spokes identify the manufacturer.

This drive sprocket lacks visible casting marks and its center cap. The use of numerous sub-contractors and regular material shortages all combined to create subtle differences in the vehicles. In order to conserve increasingly scarce rubber supplies, a new steel return roller was introduced in November of 1943. This is one of three types.

Another of the three track return roller variants was a simple, formed steel disk with lightning holes — all features designed to speed production and save material. The drive sprocket, roadwheels, and idler wheel were unchanged.

The dual roadwheels were steel stampings welded to a cast steel rim. A vulcanized, solid rubber tire was fitted to the rim. Steel tubes were inserted through holes in each face and welded to stiffen the outer edge of the whole assembly. A steel cap with a grease nipple was bolted to the center of the unit to protect the end of the axle.

The first and last roadwheel stations were equipped with shock absorbers mounted on each side of the hull. Just behind the shock absorber is the cone shaped mounting bracket for the steel return roller.

The inside face of each wheel had an extended steel lip to prevent the track guide teeth from wearing the rubber tire. Three of the steel tubes joining the wheel halves are visible in the center of the assembly. The roadwheels were 520mm (20.5 inches) in diameter with a 95mm (3.7 inch) wide tire.

13

This idler lacks the steel strips welded inside the v-shaped outer ring. The idler tension adjusting arm is visible through the spokes. Just above the roadwheel is the bump stop for the rearmost roadwheel. The bump stop consisted of a steel support and solid rubber pad and was designed to limit the travel of the wheels trailing arm. The stops were mounted above the front and rear torsion bars on each side of the hull.

A damaged StuG III has been placed aboard a flatbed recovery carrier for maintenance. The idler wheel has been removed, exposing the complete idler adjusting assembly and axle. The assembly was used to adjust the track tension — too tight and the tracks suffered from greatly accelerated wear; too loose and the tracks could come off of the vehicle.

The rear idler wheel was a complex shape consisting of fabricated steel spokes welded to a hub and two v-shaped steel rings. The inner faces of the rings have been filled in with steel strips welded in place. The outer hub was cast steel and secured in place with six bolts. A grease nipple was located in the center.

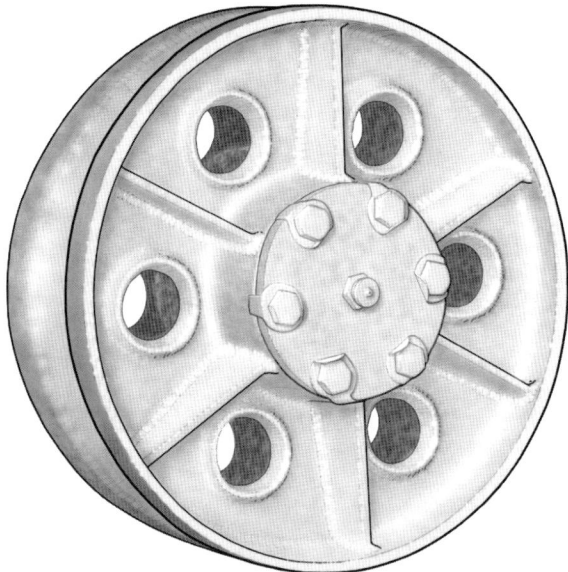

The standard rubber-tired return roller was mounted on all PzKpfw III tanks and StuG III self-propelled guns up to November of 1943. The unit consisted of two solid rubber tires bonded to two steel rims. This roller continued in use throughout 1944 until all stocks were used up.

Steel Return Roller, Third Variant

A new, all steel track return roller was introduced in late 1943 in an effort to conserve rubber. Over the course of the war, there were three types of steel return rollers. One type had six stiffening ribs radiating out from the center. The rollers were 310mm (12.2 inches) in diameter.

A second steel return roller variant had six lightening holes evenly space out around a simple steel wheel. The holes were an effort to further conserve metal and lighten the unit. The third variant was a combination of the first and last wheels and employed both stiffening ribs and lightening holes. It is unknown if they were developed in any particular order.

StuG III Ausf. Gs were equipped with a single Notek light mounted on the center of the glacis. The light was relocated to the center of the glacis from its former location on the left mudguard during production of the StuG III Ausf. F/8. It remained in this location for the Ausf. G. The bracket mounted on the face of the 30mm (1.18 inch) bolted armor plate is for stowing one of the S type tow hooks.

A gun barrel support was introduced in July of 1944. A chain and spring attached to the support would pull it aside when the barrel was elevated, thereby eliminating the need for a crewman to unnecessarily expose himself to enemy fire outside the vehicle to perform this task. It is rare to see this on an early production StuG III Ausf. G since the single 80mm front plate and the barrel support were introduced at almost the same time.

When not in use, the barrel support was folded to the right. The standard German Notek blackout night light, named after its manufacturer, *Nova-Technik GmbH* of Munich was mounted immediately to the left of the barrel support. The small hood helped to prevent the light from its 35-watt bulb from being seen from above. A new 80mm (3.15 inch) front hull plate was introduced in May of 1943, replacing the previous 50mm (1.97 inch) plate and its supplemental 30mm welded or bolted plate.

Nose Plates

Early/Middle Production:
50mm Base; 30mm Bolt-On

Middle/Late Production:
80mm Base

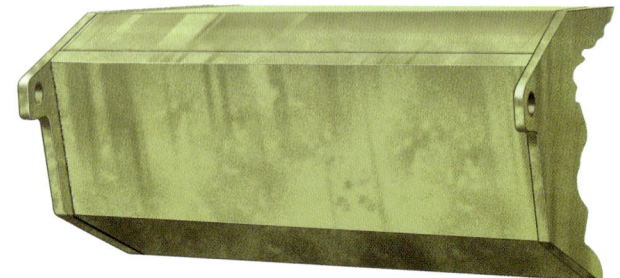

The front mudguard was riveted to a small angle that was welded to the glacis plate. The bracket on the mudguard was used to secure the vehicle's tow cable, although it was common to see the cables loosely stowed and already attached to a tow hook at the front and rear towing lugs.

Except for a limited number of StuG III Ausf. G produced on PzKpfw III Ausf. M tank hulls, all StuG III Ausf. G were equipped with two piece, side hinged glacis hatches fitted flush with the glacis plate. Those built on PzKpfw III Ausf. M hulls had two, single piece glacis hatch covers. The hinges were 'armored' to reduce the likelihood of combat damage.

One hatch included a pair of locks that were opened with a square key inserted into a hole from the outside. In order to keep out dirt and debris, a pivoting sheet metal plate covered the hole. The cover plates are missing, but their fastening rivets and one of the stops are still present. A shot deflector was mounted in front of the driver's visor, strengthened by fitting it into a recess machine into the glacis plate and securing it with recessed bolts.

This early production StuH 42 is equipped with the later 80mm glacis plates, but retains the earlier 50mm plates and 30mm bolt-on armor over the front of the fighting compartment. It also lacks the shot deflector in front of the commander's cupola. Hulls and fighting compartments were manufactured separately, which accounts for some of the mixed components.

All StuG III Ausf. G continued to use the *'Fahrersehklappe 50'* driver's visor, which was manufactured to fit in a 50mm thick armor plate. As a result, it was necessary to continue the practice of bolting a 30mm thick piece of supplemental armor onto the left side after a single 80mm plate had been adopted for the right side. This vehicle also features an interlocking weld joint for the glacis and side hull plates.

The right armor plate was augmented by 30mm thick bolt-on armor plate up to June of 1944 when the entire assembly was replaced by a single 80mm thick plate. The space behind the armor plate held an eight round ammunition bin.

The fenders, or mudguards, were manufactured using thin tread plate and strips of angled steel riveted and bolted together. The mudguards were then bolted to the hull using a L-angle strip of metal. The fittings on the mudguard are tow cable brackets.

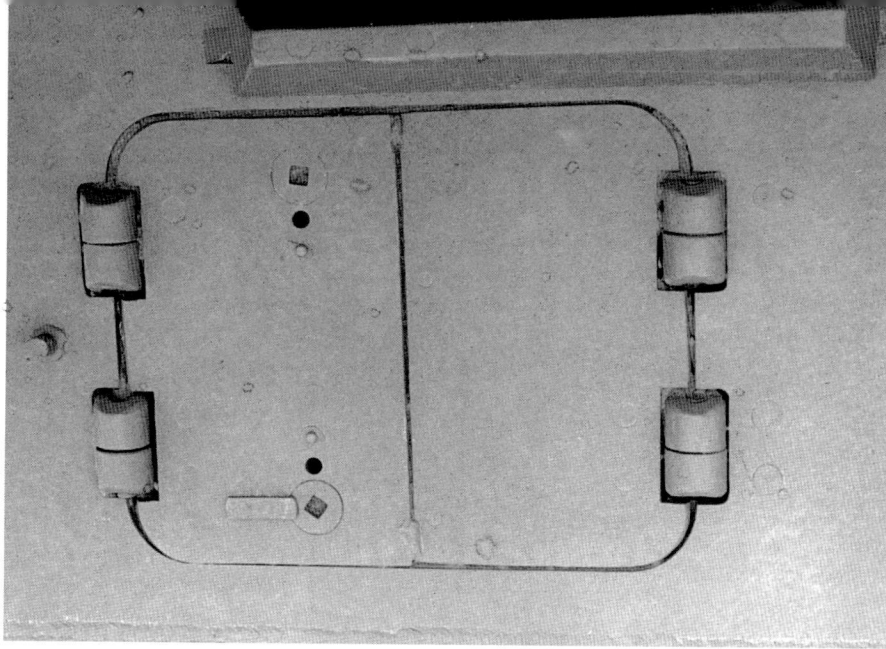

The glacis hatches were interchangeable and this example has the hatch with the locks on the left side. A short section of metal rod was welded beside the opening to keep the lip of the hatch raised, making it easier to grasp when closing the hatches.

The glacis plate hatches provided additional access to the transmission and differential units mounted in the front of the hull. The hinges and latches were mounted internally to protect them from combat damage. Theoretically, the driver could use the left hatch as an emergency exit.

The welded block mantlet, first introduced on the StuG III Ausf. F, was fitted to the Ausf. G through the end of the war. The mantlet protected the gun's recoil and recuperator components, which were mounted on top of the gun. In June of 1944, a coaxial machine gun port was added below the bolt on the upper left corner.

Russia was a dangerous place in 1944. Concrete was often used to augment the StuG III's armor, especially on those vehicles lacking the bolt-on armor. This is perhaps an extreme example — the entire front of the fighting compartment has been given a smoothly rounded coat of concrete. The crew has also augmented the armor with track links mounted across the vehicle's front and upper and lower sides.

The *'Fahrersehklappe 50'* driver's assembly contained a thick piece of armored glass in cast steel housing. The assembly was further protected by a pivoting steel cover. The driver raised and lowered the cover using two handles. Slots machined into a guide permitted the driver to select four different positions.

The driver's side vision slot was eliminated when the steeper sloped side pannier was adopted early in the production run. A pistol port, stoppered by a steel plug, was added in its place.

The front and rear mudguards were shortened and no longer hinged — both an effort to lessen production cost and time. Spare track links were often carried on the superstructure's sloping roof to improve protection.

The open glacis hatch reveals the inner hinge arrangement and lock handles. A rubber gasket, missing here, was fitted around the edge of the opening to help seal it from the elements. Part of the final drive is visible through the hatch.

The locking handles were heavy-duty castings held in place by a large nut and washer. A large coil spring between the washer and handle maintained constant pressure on the handle, preventing it from turning freely and opening by itself during vehicle operation. A sprung pin in the handle engaged a hole in the hatch when it was turned into the locked position.

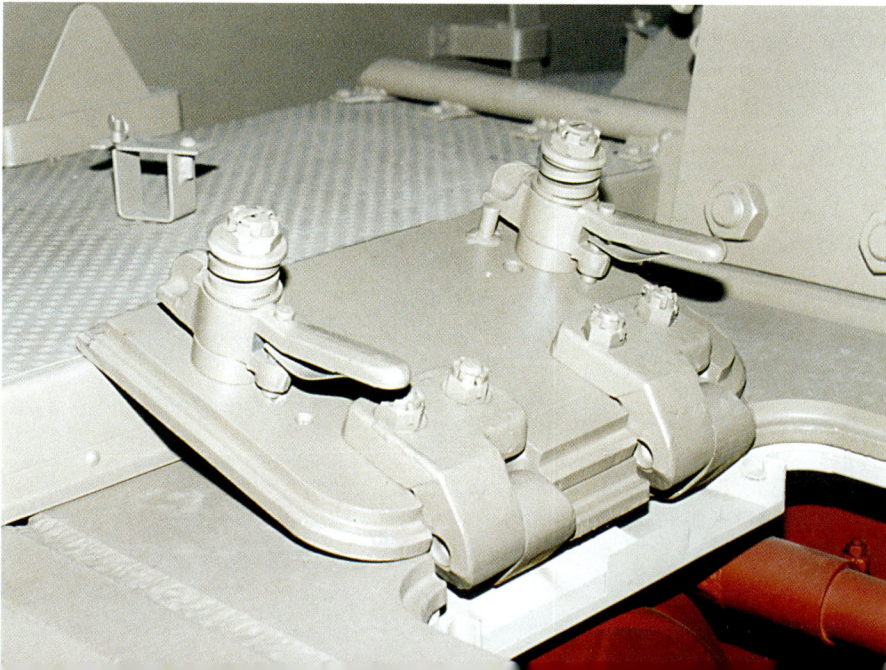

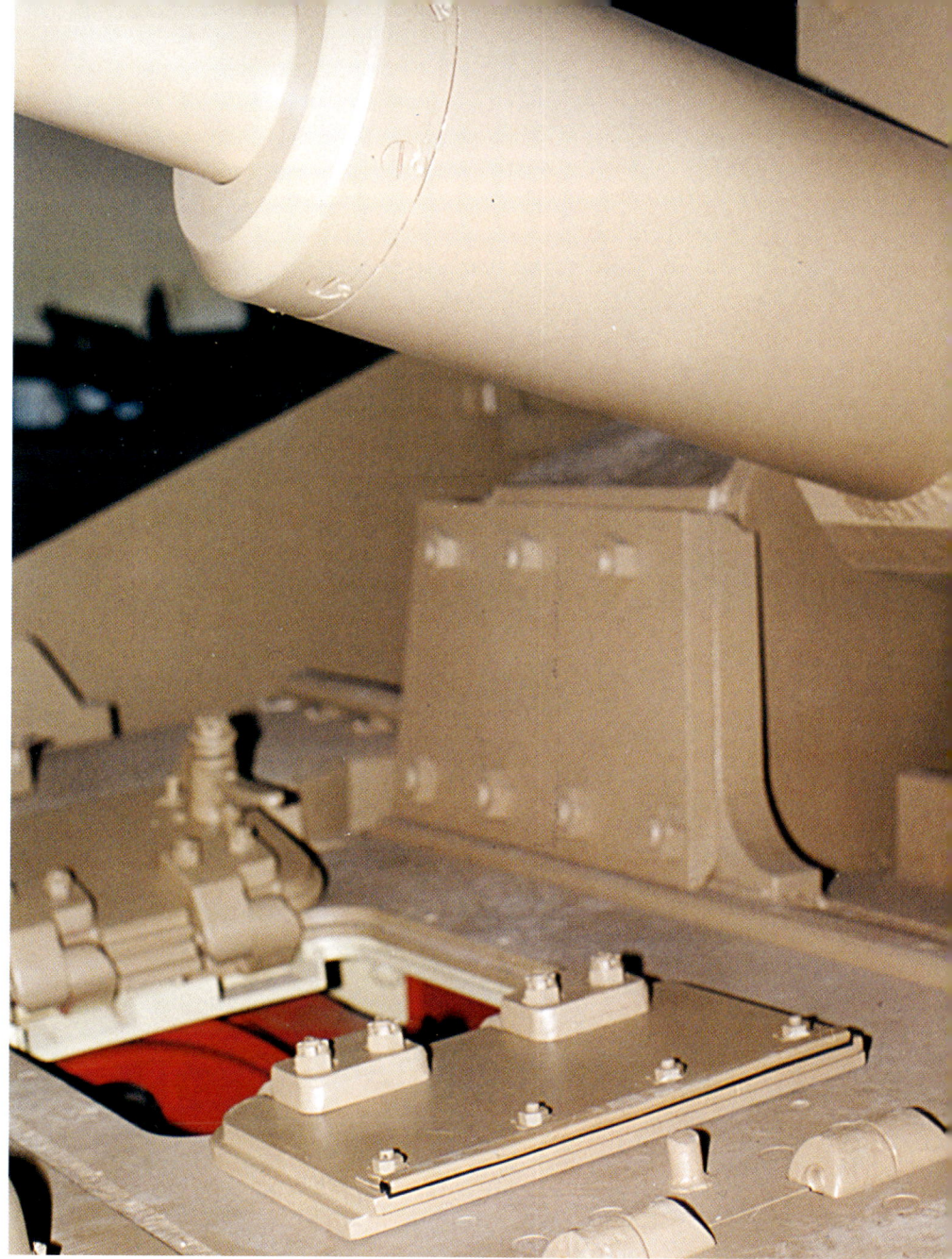

A sheet metal strip fastened to the non-locking hatch was also fitted with a rubber gasket to seal the joint between the two hatches. Both front hatches could be opened from inside the vehicle, however the right hatch was effectively blocked by the transmission and ammunition bins.

(Above Left) A great deal of labor was expended to produce the complex components of glacis hatches. Each hatch required milling to cut in the recesses for the hinges and the stepped edge.

(Above) The mantlet was set between driver's compartment on the left and ammunition stowage spaces on the right. Armored flanges welded to the driver's and ammunition compartments were designed to provide additional side protection.

(Left) The 7.5 cm StuK 40 gun had limited traverse and elevation compared to a turreted tank. The gun could traverse across a range of 20˚ and elevate from -6˚ to +20˚. The use of a muzzle brake was required; there were specific instructions that the weapon was not to be fired without it.

The sloped roof of the crew compartment and the side plates were 30MM (1.18 inches) thick while the remainder of the roof was only 10MM (0.39 inch) thick. It was not uncommon for crews to augment the armor with spare track links and, in some cases, concrete.

The 30MM bolt-on armor was mounted onto a series of threaded studs welded to the face of the armor plate. Small holes drilled through the studs allowed the nuts to be safety wired in place, although this featured does not seem to have been commonly used. Smoke grenade launchers were introduced in early 1943, but largely deleted by the late spring due to their susceptibility to damage and inadvertent activation.

The large box mantlet, made up of 45MM (1.77 inch) and 50MM (1.97 inch) plates, housed the recoil and recuperator cylinders of the 7.5 CM StuK40 main armament. A strip of armor plate was welded across the bottom of the recess to deflect any projectile from entering the fighting compartment below the mantlet.

23

A new cast gun mantlet, the *Topfblende* (pot mantlet), was introduced in November of 1943 to replace the box mantlet. Due to shortages, however, both mantlets continued to be used until the end of the war. The *Topfblende* mantlet was also known as the *Saukopf* (Pig's Head) mantlet.

The new cast gun mantlet usually had the manufacturer's cast marks near the base on the left side. The cast armor mantlet was thicker than its welded counterpart. Faint remnants of the 'waffle' pattern *Zimmerit* coating applied at the Alkett plant are visible on the sloped roof over the driver's position.

The mudguards were made of a medium gauge tread plate and held in place by both tubular and angle supports. The front and rear flaps were made of light sheet metal and easily damaged. Further back along the hull are the two L-shaped flanges used to bolt the hull and fighting compartment together.

Mantlet Casting Numbers

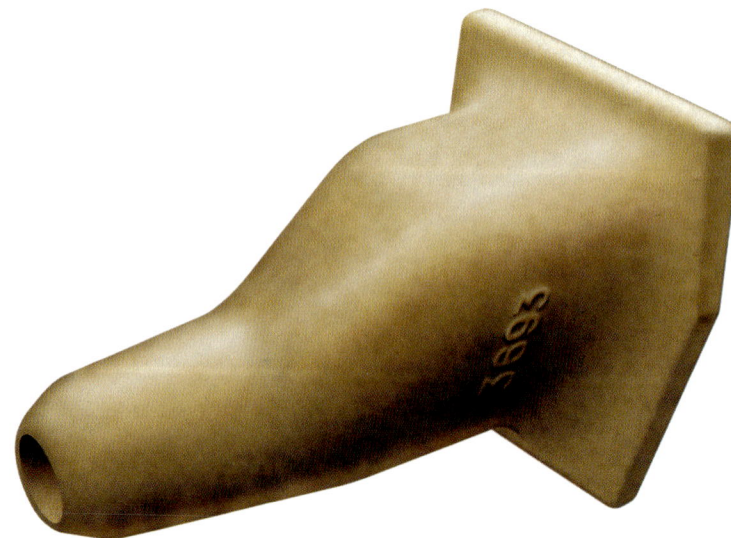

More of the old waffle pattern *Zimmerit* coating, eroded by 50 years of burial in a swamp, can be seen on the superstructure. The lines where the coating was scored stand out on the 30MM armor plate beside the gun. The cast mantlet did not receive a coat of *Zimmerit*.

A sheet metal deflector was installed under the engine deck overhang to prevent dust from being kicked up by the vehicle's powerful cooling fans. A small square fan belt inspection hatch with a domed face was installed just below the mufflers. The hatches often had a small towing clevis welded to the middle, which proved adequate for light loads such as small trailers, but was not adequate for heavier vehicles.

A small reflector hung from the left towing bracket assembly, visible just below the exhaust pipe. Each muffler was equipped with a single exhaust pipe, which vented to the outer corners of the vehicle. The fan belt inspection hatch lacks any provision for a tow pintle.

Cast Mantlet with Machine Gun Port

25

Zimmerit-coated StuG III Ausf. Gs and their crews wait for orders in France in the early spring of 1944. The cooling fan drive shaft access plates, located at the lower edge of the rear hull plate, were not coated with *Zimmerit*. All of the vehicles have the later style tubular tail light and the foreground vehicle is equipped with the late pattern 40 CM track with embossed ice cleats.

A debris screen was attached to the underside of the rear engine deck overhang immediately above the engine mufflers. Only part of the damaged dust deflector is still present on this vehicle. Small patches of *Zimmerit*, applied at the MIAG plant, are still visible below this deflector. The MIAG pattern *Zimmerit* was characterized by small dimpled squares.

StuG IIIs were factory equipped with a flat iron stowage rack wrapped around the vehicle's engine deck. There were regular instances of the vehicles leaving the factory without it owing to shortages of time or material. Some units cobbled their own racks together. Panzer Grenadiers also used the rack as a handhold when riding on the vehicle.

The fan belt inspection hatch was eliminated at some time during the middle of production. The small chain and clip hanging off the broken tow bracket was used to hold a steel bar inserted through the tow eyes. The round plate under the tail provided lubrication access to the cooling fan drive shaft.

This right side muffler is dented, but otherwise undamaged. The inner end was angled to clear the fan belt inspection plate. The two small brackets welded to the muffler were used to attach the sheet metal dust deflector.

Later StuG III Ausf. Gs deleted the fan belt inspection plate and added a heavy duty towing pintle across the rear hull plate. This vehicle also retains its stowage/grab rail around the engine deck. The welded rail assembly was bolted to small pads tack welded to the engine deck.

The exhaust pipes wrapped over the top of the rear hull plate before descending into the mufflers. Two of the braces that support the rear plate and the mount for the vehicle's engine crank are also visible. This area was normally painted the same color as the vehicle exterior — Panzer Yellow (approximately FS33434).

27

(Above Left) The original colors and markings are still visible on the rear plate of this late StuG III Ausf. G — unusual in that the *Balkenkreuz* (Beam Cross) is outlined in red instead of white. The emblem has not yet been identified as that of any specific *Sturmgeschütz Abteilung* (Assault Gun Battalion).

(Above) The 50mm rear plate on this vehicle is welded to the side plates with an interlocking joint. The debris screen is bolted to lugs welded to the hull plate lower edges just below the engine deck overhang.

(Left) A new horizontal tow bar was installed on StuG III Ausf. G beginning in late 1944. It was designed to be used with tow bars, which provided more control when towing another vehicle, especially downhill. The round engine crank cover plate is hanging open at the top. The white stenciling was applied after the vehicle was recovered and is not original.

(Above) The unit emblem is a red dog or wolf head in a white shield outlined in red. The rear reflector attached to the tow hold is just visible at lower left. The red reflector was easily covered by dust and mud.

(Above Right) Later StuG III Ausf. Gs were equipped with a steel frame welded to the engine deck to help contain the crew's belongings and provide a handhold for Panzer Grenadiers. In order to gain more space on the engine deck, the spare roadwheel mounts were often relocated to a steel plate welded to the side of the frame. The two outer rear plate supports were eliminated on late StuG III Ausf. G. Additionally, only two cone head bolts were used to secure them.

(Right) This StuG III Ausf. G still has the four support plates each with three cone head bolts. This is likely a later production hull as evidenced by the interlocking weld joints and the two groups of castellated nuts used to secure the late style tow pintle.

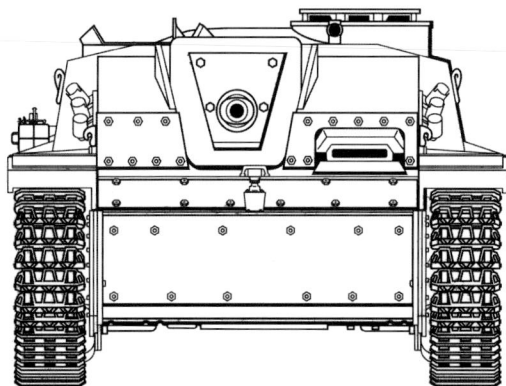

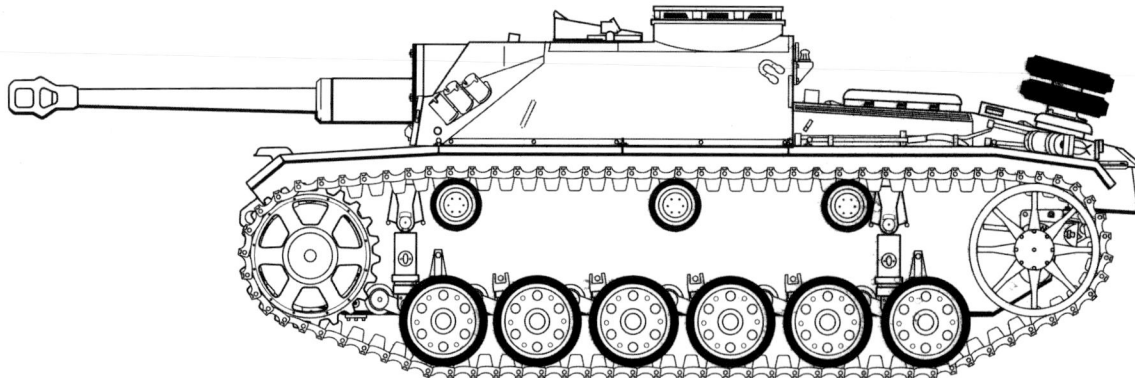

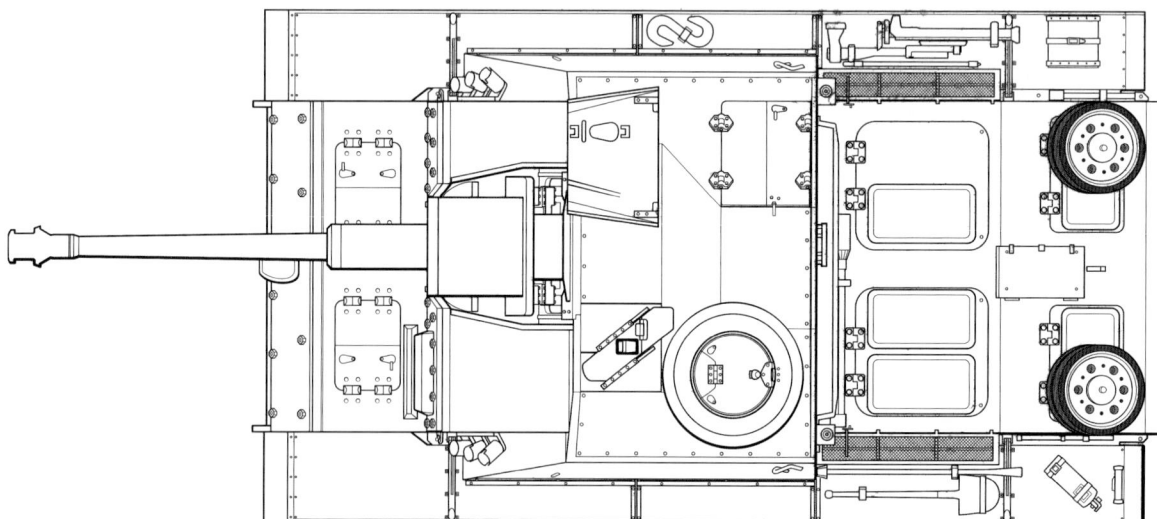

Sturmgeschütz III Ausf. G (Early) (Sd.Kfz 142/1) Specifications

Length:..................21.98 feet (6.7 m)

Width:....................9.68 feet (2.95 m)

Height:..................7.22 feet (2.2 m)

Empty Weight:......47,899 pounds (21,727 kg)

Loaded Weight:....57,098.8 pounds (25,846.1 kg)

Powerplant:..........One 265 hp Maybach HL 120 TRM V-12 12-cylinder, liquid-cooled engine

Transmission:......SSG 77 – Six speeds forward, one speed reverse

Armament:............One hull-mounted 7.5 cm StuK 40 gun with 54 rounds, and one roof-mounted 7.92mm MG34 machine gun with 600 rounds

Maximum Speed:.24.86 mph (40 kmh)

Range:..................96.3 miles (155 km)

Crew:....................Four

The rear tow pintles were steel castings that also served as mounts for the track-tensioning rod. A large bolt head on the end of the rod allowed it to be turned with a wrench. The other end of the rod was threaded through an arm on the idler mount, which moved back and forth, pivoting the idler wheel and tightening or loosening the tracks.

The mudguard supports were secured to the L-angles used to bolt the engine deck to the lower hull. The rearmost support ran under the mudguard, while the tubular support ran over the top.

The mudguard support channel is missing on this example allowing a clear view of the L-shaped angles used to attach the upper and lower hull components. The mudguard support channel was attached with two bolts and fit through the notch in the double angles.

There was a large gap behind the mantlet that exposed the interior of the crew compartment to the elements. This was often closed up with a canvas cover. The cap is a replica of an *Einheitsfeldmütze* manufactured in September of 1943. The field gray cap was standard issue.

A piece of the box mantlet has been shot away, cracking the weld joint and providing a view of the gun trunnion and recoil mechanisms. The center section of the opening through the front of the superstructure could be removed to permit the gun's removal.

Bolted connections attach the mantlet to the gun trunnions. This method was also used on the welded mantlet. Small bent clips welded to the back of the mantlet and front of the removable bar were used to secure the canvas weather shield.

Mantlet Cover

Although the introduction of armored side skirts (*Schürzen*) proved to be an effective way of protecting the vehicles against Russian anti-tank rifles, the skirts method of attachment was inadequate, often resulting in the loss of the plates. In March of 1944, a second style of *Schürzen* mounts were introduced which used triangular plates combined with brackets welded to the inside face of the plates.

The lower brackets were bolted to the mudguards. The upper brackets were attached to an L-angle rail that was in turn bolted to three brackets attached to the crew compartment and engine deck.

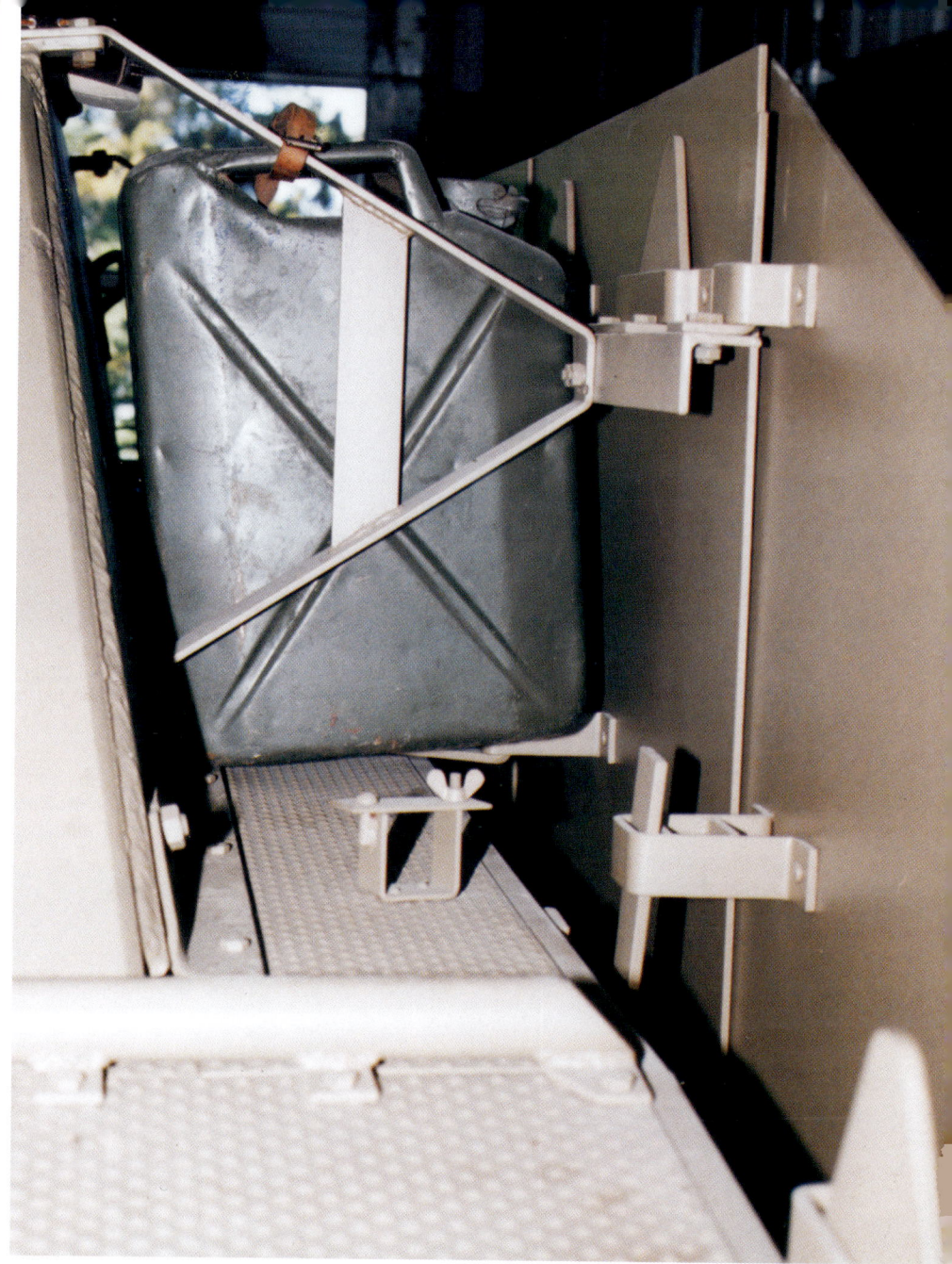

The brackets on the *Schürzen* were riveted to the thin (approximately 5mm) steel plates. The upper bracket supported the weight of the skirt at a fixed distance from the hull. The lower brackets were designed to allow the skirts to be adjusted at a variable distance from the running gear — important if the vehicle was equipped with the wider *Ostketten* or *Winterketten* tracks.

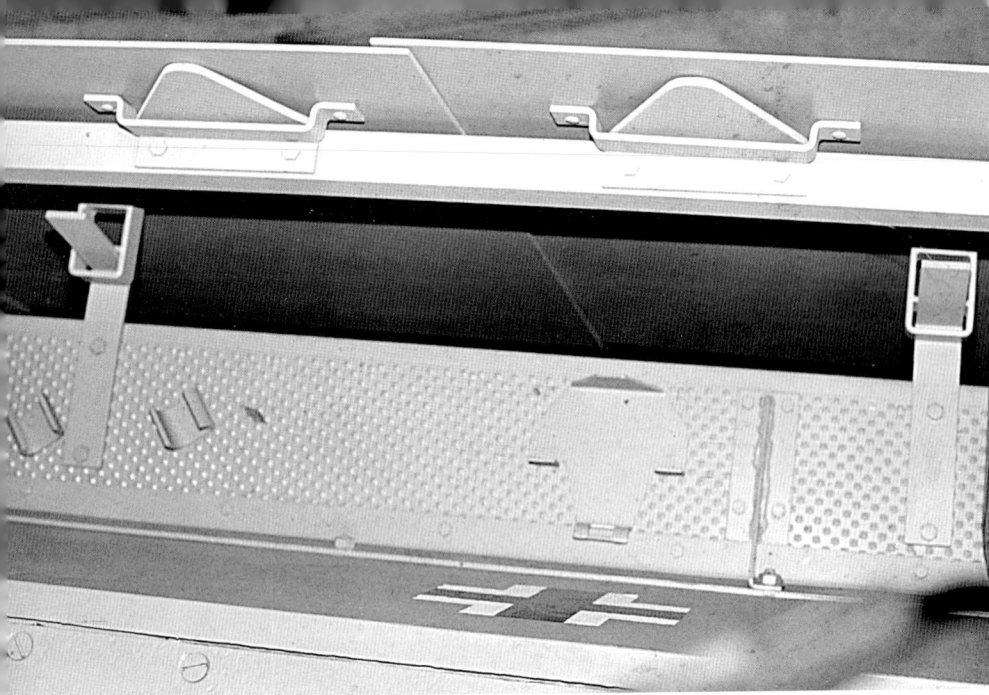

The wide bracket on the mudguard is for stowing a 'C' tow hook. It is missing the clamp attached to the outside edge. The two C-shaped clamps tack welded to the mudguard were used to secure the loop in the tow cable.

Some StuG III Ausf. Gs also carried an extra layer of skirt plates mounted over the main skirts. This layer was only half the depth of the main skirts and was designed to provide an extra measure of protection to the fighting compartment. The skirts were effective against anti-tank rifle rounds, small arms fire, and shrapnel.

The skirts were less effective against large caliber high explosive (HE) or anti-tank rounds — as evidenced by the torn and bent rear skirt. This is an earlier production Ausf. G with the full range of bolt-on armor and no shot deflector in front of the commander's cupola.

This later production vehicle has the 80mm (3.15 inch) glacis plates, bolt-on fighting compartment armor, a *Topfblende* mantlet with cover, and a shot deflector in front of the commander's cupola. It is also wearing side skirts and Alkett's waffle pattern *Zimmerit*.

The StuG III Ausf. G employed two primary types of muzzle brakes — round and a flattened oval. The only difference between the two is the machining across the top and bottom of the foremost baffles to give it an elliptical shape.

One of the types of muzzle brake used on the StuH 42 was this one originally designed for the 10.5 CM IFH18/M howitzer. It featured two wide flanges on either side to further reduce the recoil forces on the lighter 7.5 CM PaK40 gun carriage that was also used as a mount for the howitzer.

The side flanges were added in May of 1943 to help reduce the amount of dust and smoke raised after firing, a factor which could impede further target observation. The muzzle brake was threaded on to the end of the barrel and secured with a tightening bolt on the top and a locking collar at the rear. This muzzle brake is installed upside down.

This example of the StuH 42 muzzle with the extra-wide baffles is mounted on the *Geschützwagen* 39H(f) at Saumur. Muzzle brakes were complicated, time consuming, and costly castings to produce. By July of 1944, muzzle brakes were eliminated from some guns including the 10.5 CM StuH 42.

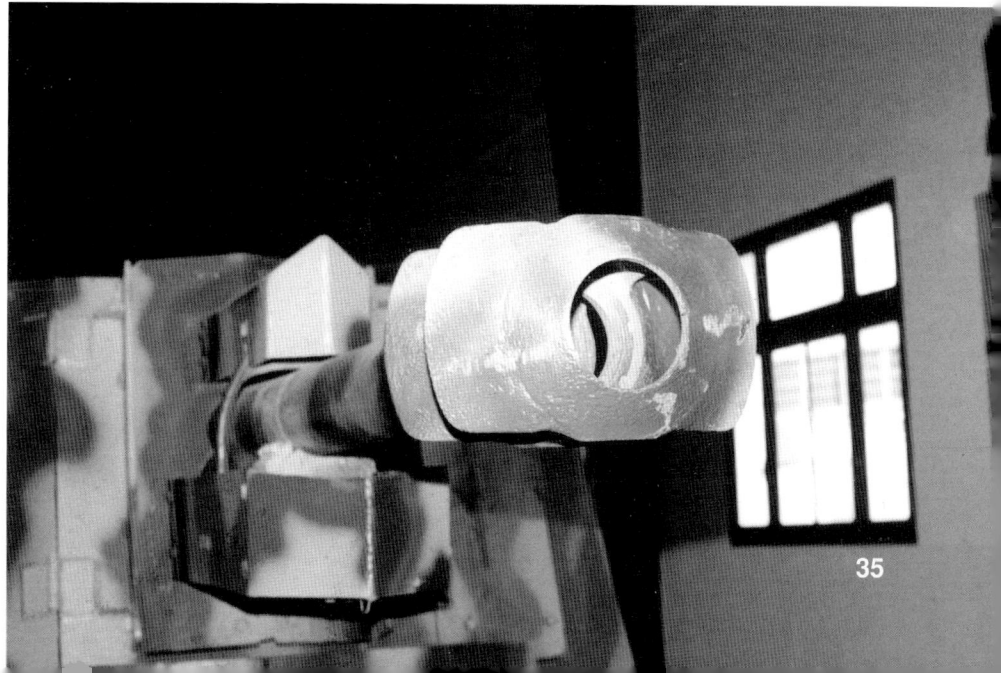

(Above Left) This muzzle brake and its locking collar are in the proper position. The collar was tightened against the back of the brake to hold it securely in place.

(Above) The spare roadwheel mounts have been relocated to steel plates welded to the side of the engine deck and stowage/grab rail. This was a common field modification and provided the crew with more space on the engine deck to stow their belongings. The end of the mount was threaded inside and the wheel was held in place by means of a round cap plate and bolt.

(Left) The mudguards adjacent to the air intakes were cut out to provide clearance. Part of the mudguard was bent up 90° for the length of the intake housing to reinforce the opening. Several late war additions are visible in this photograph: the cupola shot deflector, a *Pilze** mount for the 2-ton jib crane, and two small hooks attached to an angle beside the fume extraction ventilator that secured the engine deck hatches when they were raised. The two 'C' brackets on the mudguard held the tow cable in place. Just to the right, the small triangular fitting held the end of the pry bar. The clamps for these last two pieces of equipment are missing.

*Literally, mushroom, although its German Army connotation in this instance is uncertain.

(Above) The forward jack mount was bolted to the right mudguard. A large wing nut on the threaded rod hanging down from the bracket top secured the outside hinged part of the bracket (missing on this example). The mounting brackets for the engine crank are welded to the side of engine air intake. The end of the crank fit into the short round tube and the handle into the larger clamp towards the front.

(Right) Spare radio antennas were held in place by the angle bracket with the three tubes. The tip of the antenna slid into the long tube, while the base was attached to a shorter rod on the opposite side of the engine deck. The two shorter rods on this side supported the bases of two more antennas, although there was only space for one tip on the opposite side. Spare tracks were normally carried on the rear wall of the crew compartment. The square wire mesh over the engine air intake is a post-war addition.

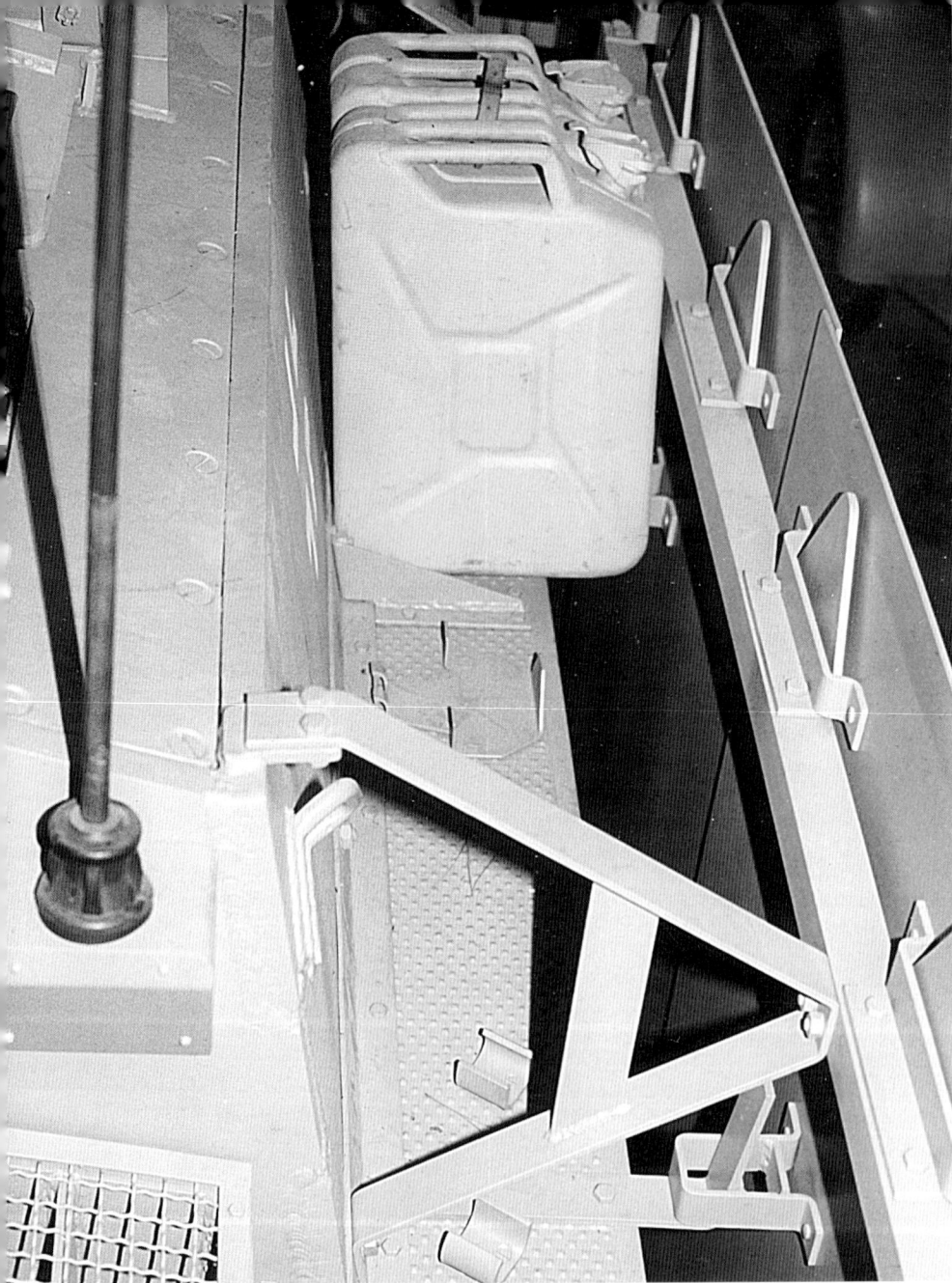

The *Schürzen* mounting brackets were bolted to a short length of flat steel welded to the fighting compartment side plate, while the lower end was secured with a mudguard mounting bolt. The addition of *Schürzen* provided a convenient stowage space for all sorts of equipment such as the jerrycans shown here.

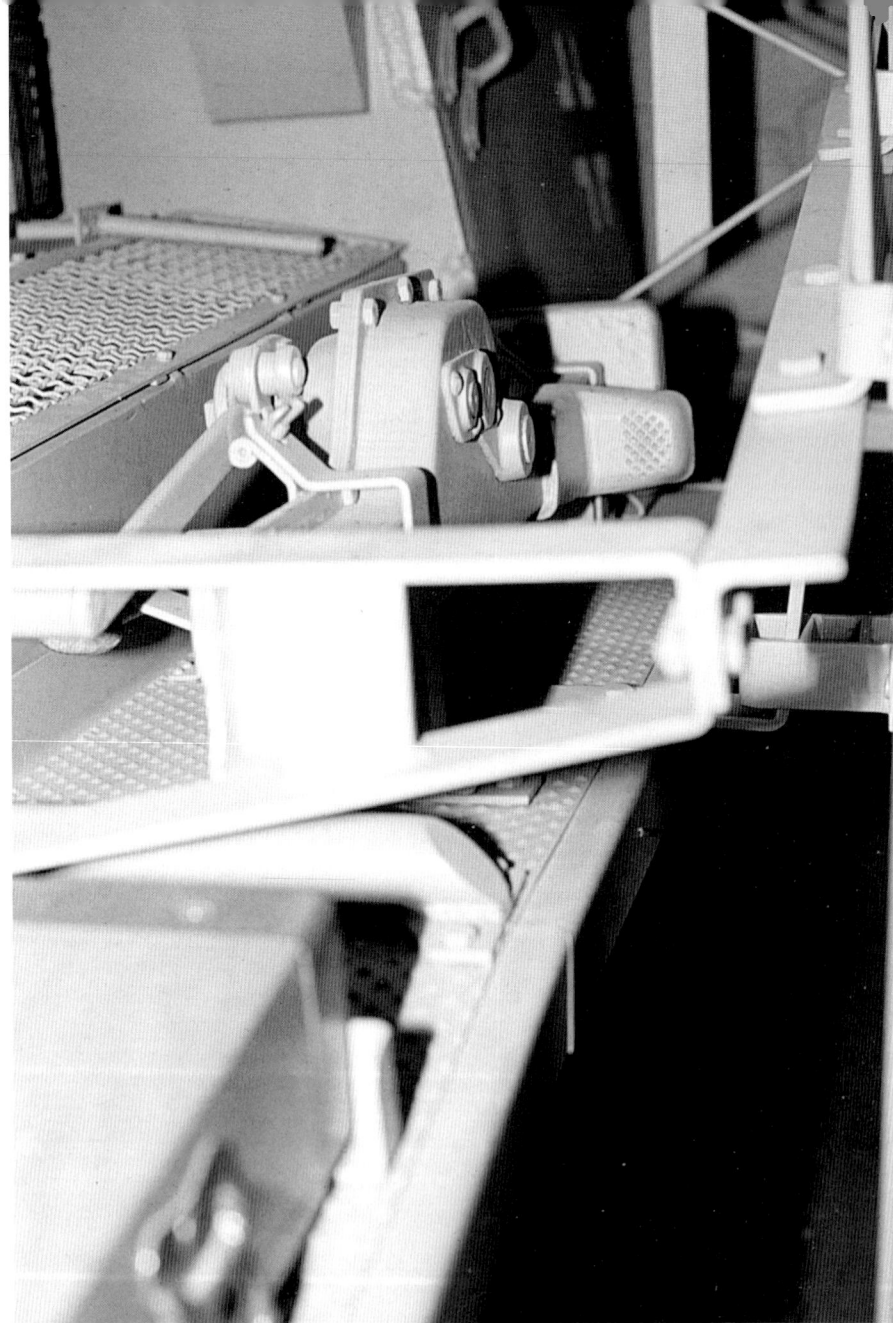

The vehicle jack was located on the right mudguard next to the engine air intake. The Germans used a wide variety of jacks on their armored vehicles. The jacks were generally similar, but differed in small details and lifting capacity over the course of the war.

The wire mesh screen over the engine air intakes is original on this vehicle. It was a woven wire, similar to modern chain link fencing. The spare antenna mount can be seen here as well, although the tube for the tip has been broken off. It is obvious that there is not space for a third antenna. The box shaped bracket held the ends of the four gun barrel cleaning rods.

The hinged bracket in the center held the other end of the barrel cleaning rods. The small inverted U-shaped bracket beside it provided support for the two spare antennas. A large circular steel plate covered the fume extraction ventilator on the rear of the crew compartment. The L-shaped bracket is one of three vertical straps welded to the engine deck — a field modification believed to be used to secure a wooden stowage crate.

The antenna mount on the left side was different than that on the right side. It was narrower and the mounting bolts were on the outside of the mount. The upper portion of the hard rubber antenna base has been broken off.

The antenna mount on the right side was wider and the mounting bolts for it were inside the mount. A thin sheet metal cover was screwed to the back face to protect the cable that ran through a hole in the back wall of the crew compartment. The remains of the axe brackets are visible on the mudguard.

(Above Left) Small triangular plates bolted to the mounting rail were used to secure the *Schürzen* plates at the top. The bottom of the *Schürzen* was secured with a U shaped bracket that fit over a bent flat strap bolted to the mudguard. The bottom of the *Schürzen* could be moved in or out depending on which space the bottom strap was placed in. This was necessary when *Ostketten* or *Winterketten* tracks were used.

(Above) The antenna mount was made of hard rubber with a post in the middle. The antenna had a split tube base which was slipped over the post and tightened with a wing nut clamp. Two vented hatches were set into the engine deck.

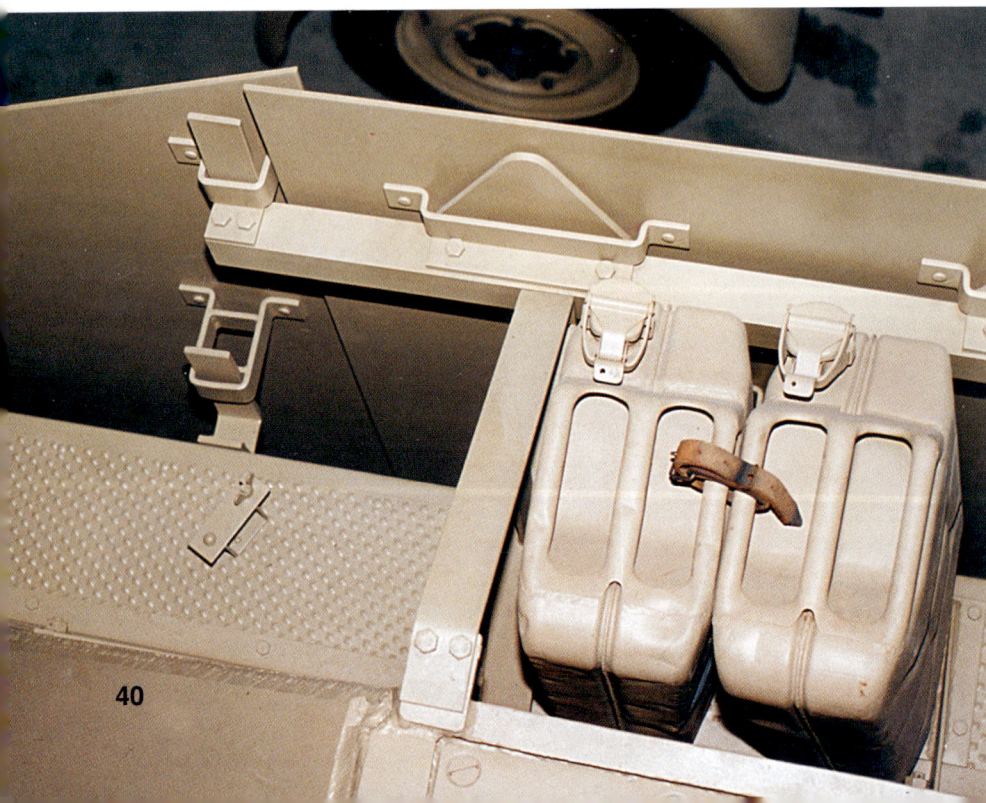

(Left) The front skirt used a simple L-shaped bracket bolted to the rail. The front skirt's forward mount was attached to the mudguard. The rail mounts were bolted to the fighting compartment sides. Each side skirt was slightly overlapped by the skirt in front of it.

The gun barrel cleaning rod brackets were located behind the crew compartment on the forward part of the engine deck along with the spare antenna stowage brackets. The antenna mount on the left side is for the FuG (*Funkgerät*; Radio Device) 15 USW receiver used by the vehicle commander. The mount on the right is for the FuG 16 USW receiver and 10 watt transmitter used by the loader/radio operator.

The antenna rod slipped over a metal post in a molded, hard rubber base, which was attached to the U-shaped mount. The antenna wire ran under the mount into a small hole in the fighting compartment's rear wall. The spare antenna rod mount on the engine deck is set up to hold two spare antenna rods.

The engine deck was equipped with two vented hatches to provide routine engine maintenance. The rectangular hatch openings were capped by armored covers. The entire engine deck could be lifted off the vehicle if it was necessary to change the engine.

Both opened engine hatches reveal their rectangular ventilation slots. A pair of hatches on the rear of the engine deck allowed access to the radiator fans. This StuG III Ausf. G is in Rumanian service on the Eastern Front.

Removing the engine meant removing the entire engine deck. The StuG III Ausf. G was powered by a 265 HP Maybach HL 120 TRM V-12 engine. A 310 L (81.89 gallon) gasoline tank was located in the engine compartment directly behind the loader.

German mechanics disassemble the valve train on a StuG III Ausf. G. The vehicle's engine deck has been removed exposing one of the large cooling fans. Once disconnected, the engine was hoisted out of the engine compartment. In addition to the PzKpfw III and StuG III vehicles, the Maybach HL 120 TRM also powered most variants of the PzKpfw IV medium tank.

Spare track links were stowed on the rear wall of the crew compartment. A channel rail attached to a bracket with a swivel bolt and butterfly nut secured the tracks to the wall. The track links also provided an additional measure of protection against increasingly larger Allied anti-tank guns.

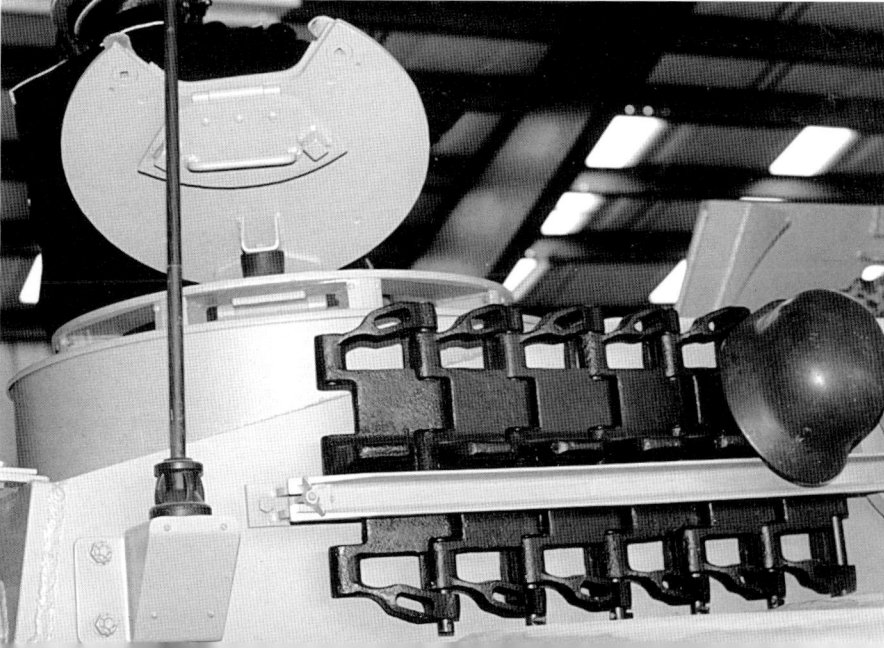

Wire cutters — a standard piece of equipment on German armored vehicles — were mounted on the left rear side of the engine deck. The Z-shaped bracket just behind the engine air intake supported one of the handles, while the cutting end was secured with the two-piece clamp at the rear. The rear Notek light was mounted on the left mudguard. This damaged bracket held one of the later tubular style lights.

The 50MM (1.97 inch) rear plate is interlocked with the side plate on this vehicle. Interlocking the plates on later production vehicles made the plates less prone to coming apart when hit. Two L-angle strips were used to attach the superstructure and engine deck to the lower hull and make them easier to remove for maintenance and repairs. The armor plate on the upper engine deck was only 30MM (1.18 inch) thick.

43

The engine deck arrangement of the StuG III Ausf. G was the same as that of the PzKpfw III Ausf. L. Three large rectangular cover plates over holes in the engine deck hatches provided ventilation to the engine compartment. The hatches on the rearmost were located over the two powerful cooling fans serving the vehicle's radiators. Two spare roadwheel mounts are bolted to the fan covers. The four vertical straps (the left one is missing, but the weld bead is still visible) were a field modification believed to be used to secure a wooden crate on the engine deck.

The spare roadwheel mounts have been relocated to the side of the crew compartment on this StuH 42 Ausf. G. This was not a common arrangement. This vehicle is also equipped with the remote control machine gun mount and the side opening loader's hatches. Both features were introduced in April of 1944.

The StuG III's mudguards were used to hold a variety of spare tools and equipment. Brackets for the spade (left) and pry bar (right) were mounted on the left mudguard adjacent to the engine intake. The diamond-shaped, woven wire mesh over the air intake is original.

Beginning in February of 1943, two smoke grenade launcher racks were installed on the forward sides of the superstructure. They consisted of three tubes arranged in a pattern designed to launch smoke grenades across the front of the vehicle.

The tubes were fired electrically from inside the vehicle. These smoke grenade launchers are mounted on a PzKpfw III. The wires passed through a small hole in the armor.

The launcher tubes were thin sheet metal and were susceptible to damage from small arms fire that could set off the grenade in the tube. Crew complaints resulted in the smoke launchers elimination in May of 1943.

The superstructure was bolted to the lower hull by means of a double angle that ran down both sides of the hull just below the mudguard. Cotter pins held the lower castellated nuts in place, while the upper bolts were held in place by a thin washer bent up along the side of the nut.

The engine air intake extended down to the lower hull and was joined to the lower hull angle. This feature was present on both PzKpfw IIIs and StuG IIIs.

The engine deck cover plates were stamped from 16mm steel plate. This made the edges uneven and slightly beveled.

Eight periscopes were positioned around the commander's cupola. Each periscope was faced with a clear plexiglas cover, secured with a metal plate and four screws, to protect the periscope from the elements.

Early cupolas lacked any means of shot deflection and were susceptible to damage or penetration by anti-tank rounds. Spare track links were often used to improve ballistic protection in the field.

A shot deflector was introduced in front of the commander's cupola in October of 1943. Made from stamped steel plate, it was welded to the face of the cupola and roof of the crew compartment.

The wedged-shaped shot deflector greatly improved the cupola's protection. The commander's hatch was hinged up and to the rear. A small flap at the hatch front allowed use of a scissors periscope. Later production StuG IIIs replaced the recessed roof mounting screws with simple bolts. A *Pilze* socket for a 2-ton jib crane is welded to the roof behind the cupola.

This late model hatch is fitted with a handle to assist the commander in closing it through the cupola without exposing himself to enemy fire. The two ends were bent at 90° and when lifted perpendicular to the hatch face, provided the necessary leverage to swing the hatch closed. The center of the hatch was normally padded to protect the commander's head from injury.

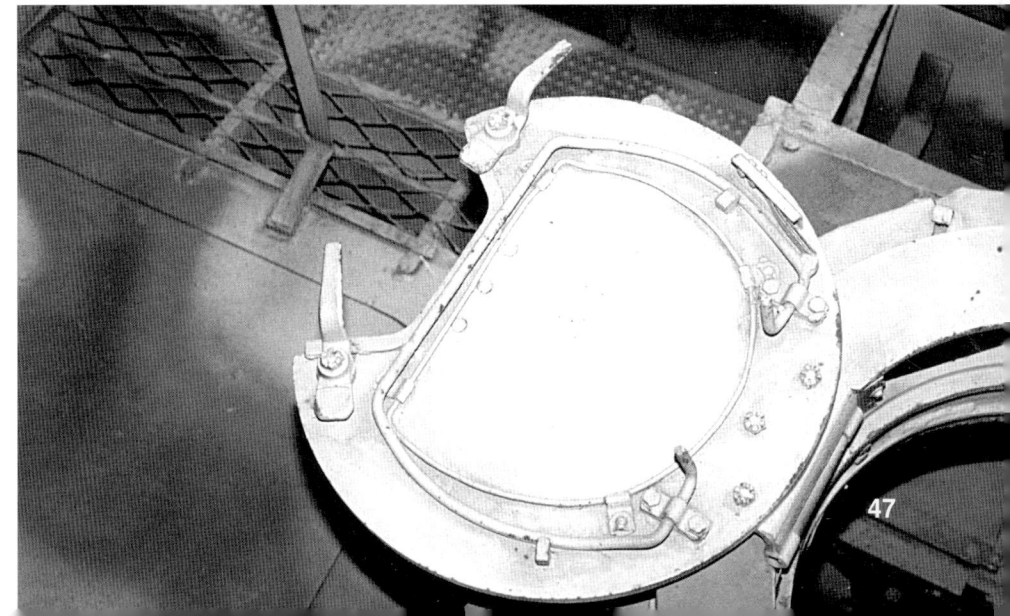

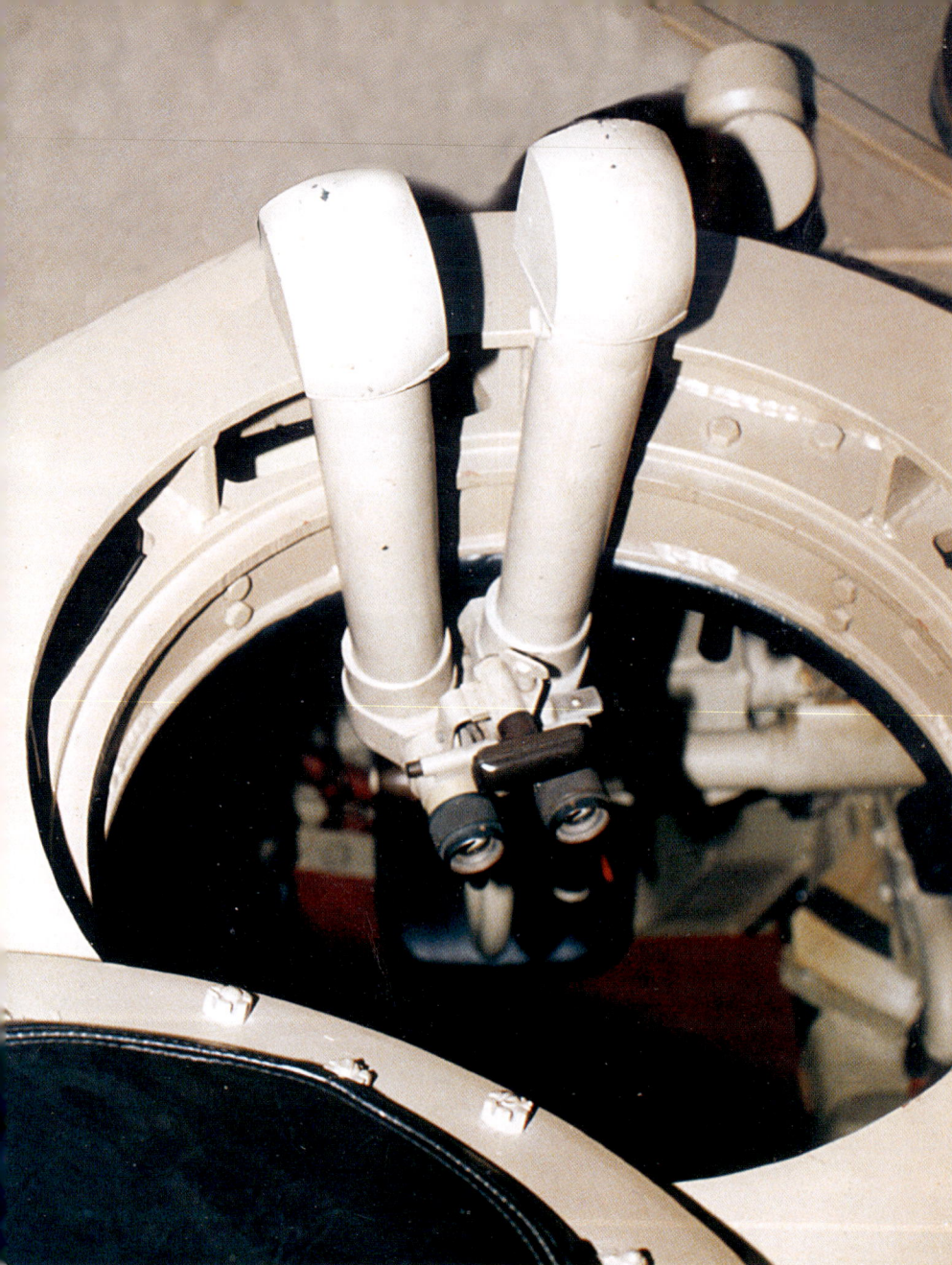

This cupola hatch has a stop that prevented it from opening a full 180°. A small rubber bumper was normally attached to the stop using a welded bolt. Later production vehicles stopped using the rubber stops due to increasingly scarce rubber supplies. This is an earlier production vehicle and lacks the shot deflector.

The SflZF1c (*Selbstfahrlafetten-Zielfernrohr 1c*) gun sight projected through the roof of the crew compartment. It was surrounded by a sliding cover joined to the gun. Both the sight and cover plate moved with the gun when it was traversed.

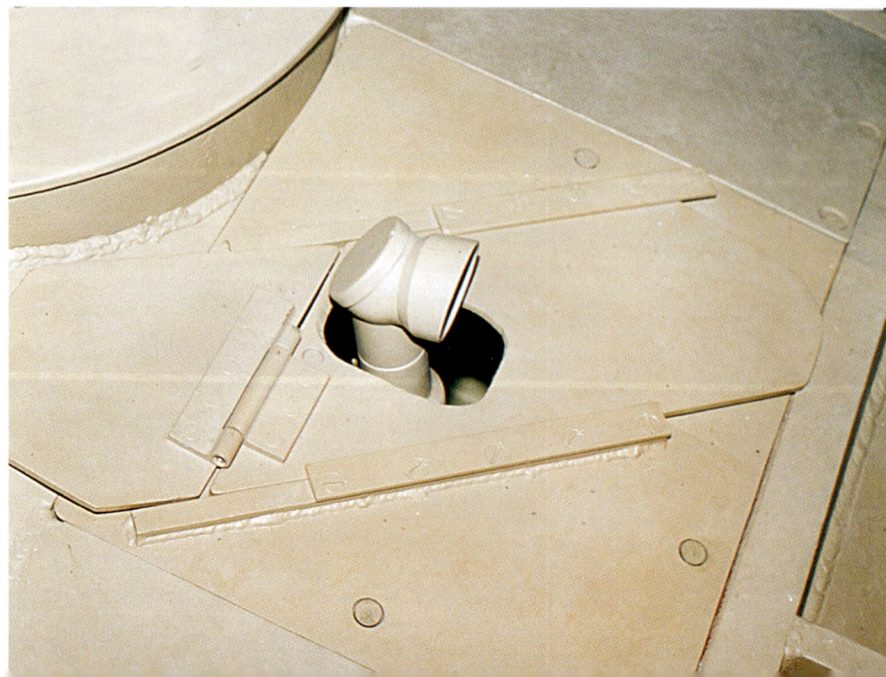

The *Scherenfernrohr* 14 scissors periscope could be mounted in the cupola and used with the hatch open or closed. This device allowed the commander to observe the battlefield without having to expose himself, as he would have to do with ordinary binoculars. Padding was applied to the hatch interior, protecting the commander's head in case he bumped it against the hatch while inside the vehicle.

The machine gun shield was bolted to a simple hinge that allowed it to fold down when not in use. The shields were normally folded forward to prevent interference with the loader's hatches.

The machine gun was attached to the shield with a special mount that fit into a slotted bracket welded to the shield. A second bracket was welded to the top edge of the shield. The drum magazine on this 7.92ᴍᴍ MG42 held 50 rounds.

The machine gun shield was held in place using a flat strap on the front hatch to engage a rod welded to the shield. The opening in the front of this shield was originally designed to be used with the 7.92ᴍᴍ MG34 machine gun. Shields designed for the later MG42 employed a rectangular opening. Both weapons could be used in either shield.

A machine gun shield was introduced in December of 1942 and used on all new StuG III Ausf. G. It was hinged and could be laid flat when not in use. There were two mounts for the MG34 or MG42 fixed to the back, one for use against ground targets below the cut out and one for aerial use at the top of the shield. The shield only provided protection for the gunner from the front. This is the later shield with the rectangular opening designed primarily for use with the MG42.

Late Upper Hull

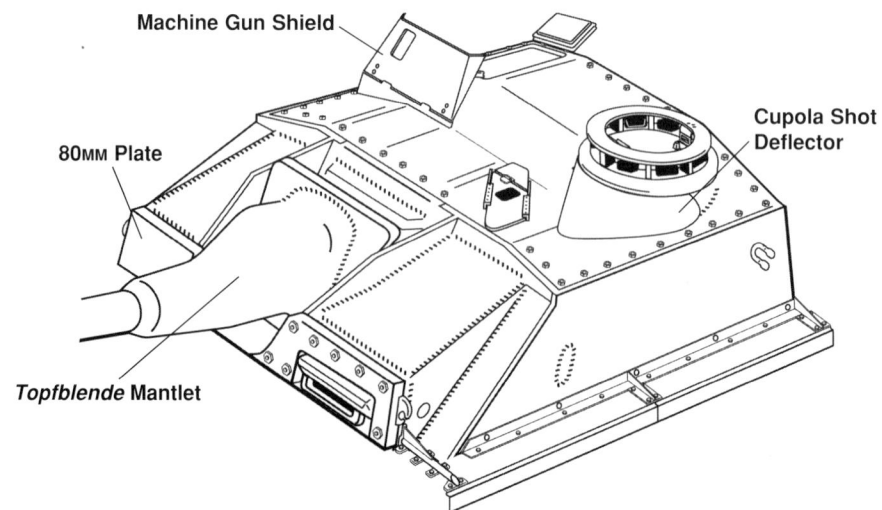

The *Scherenfernrohr* 14 scissors periscope could be dismounted and used off the vehicle. This particular StuG III Ausf. G was based in Italy with *Sturmgeschütz Abteilung* (Assault Gun Battalion) 242, attached to the Hermann Göring Division.

Machine Gun Shield

Cupola Shot Deflector

80ᴍᴍ Plate

Topfblende Mantlet

The wooden jack block was mounted on the right rear mudguard. Two angle brackets and a leather strap held it in place on the mudguard.

A small, open box held the sledgehammer's head in place on the side of the engine deck. A clamp held the handle. Remnants of the schürzen bracket are visible just above the hammer mount. This vehicle also employs a later style mudguard support. The triangular flange was designed to increase the strength of the support as more and heavier equipment was stowed on the mudguards.

The axe was held in place using a sheet metal bracket bent to shape. The turned over lip on the outside edge secured the sharp edge of the axe with the back of the head facing the hull. The clamp beside it held the handle, while the handle end was held in place by the U-shaped bracket to the right.

Last Upper Hull

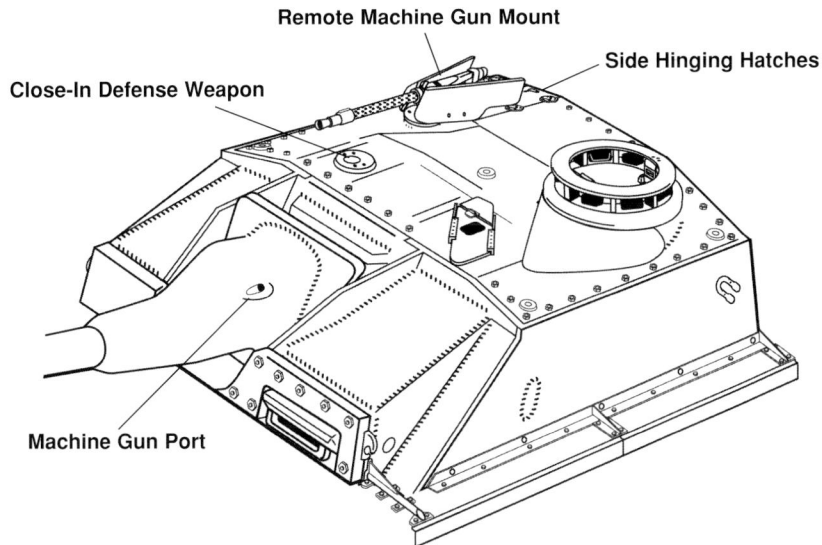

Close-In Defense Weapon

Remote Machine Gun Mount

Side Hinging Hatches

Machine Gun Port

A remote control MG34 machine gun mount with a wrap-around shield was introduced in April of 1944. It could be fired from inside the vehicle by the loader/radio operator with complete protection. A mechanism in the mount allowed a small degree of elevation and depression of the weapon.

The remote control machine gun mount was equipped with a periscopic sight providing a 3x magnification and an 8° field of vision. This mount is on a *Jagdpanzer* 38(t) Hetzer self-propelled anti-tank gun.

StuG IIIs employed in the command vehicle role were equipped with additional radios. This is the large antenna mount for the FuG 8 command radio with its special armored housing. The hard rubber mount has six fins whereas the smaller mounts for the FuG 15 and FuG 16 only had four fins. It is attached to a large porcelain insulator at the base. A similar mount was also employed on later PzKpfw IV command tanks.

Most German tanks were equipped with a hardwood jack block. The ends were wrapped with a steel strap to prevent the wood from splitting and each block was equipped with a handle. This block is a replica of the original.

The jack block was stowed in an angle bracket on the right rear mudguard of the StuG III Ausf. G and held in place by a leather belt attached to a steel wire loop on the front. The other end was hooked to a clasp fixed to the angle bracket. Jack blocks were used to prevent the jack from sinking into soft ground.

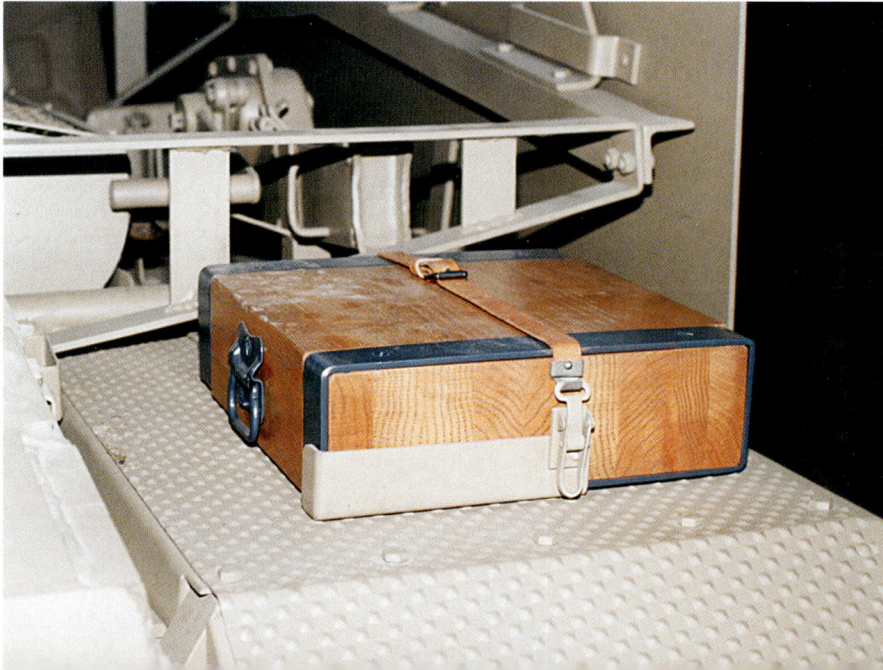

Prominent weld beads and roughly finished edges on the armor plate were common on the StuG III. This magnificently restored vehicle has the interlocking hull armor plates. The clasp for the small sledgehammer is missing from its base.

53

StuG III Ausf. Gs prepare to move out in southern Russia in 1943. The engine cranks on these vehicles are mounted on the engine air intakes. The axe is secured in it position on the mudguard, just below the engine crank. Just behind the axe is the early style mudguard support.

This early production Ausf. G is also equipped with the early mudguard supports as well as the early Notek rear lamp. This vehicle, on display at Aberdeen Proving Ground, Maryland, has had its fighting compartment armor cut apart for testing. It was welded back together for display purposes.

This weather-beaten Ausf. G awaits restoration. Surprisingly, most of its easily damaged tool and equipment mounting brackets appear to be intact: the axe and jacket brackets on the mudguard and the engine crank clamp on the air intake. This vehicle used the earlier recessed screws to secure the fighting compartment roof.

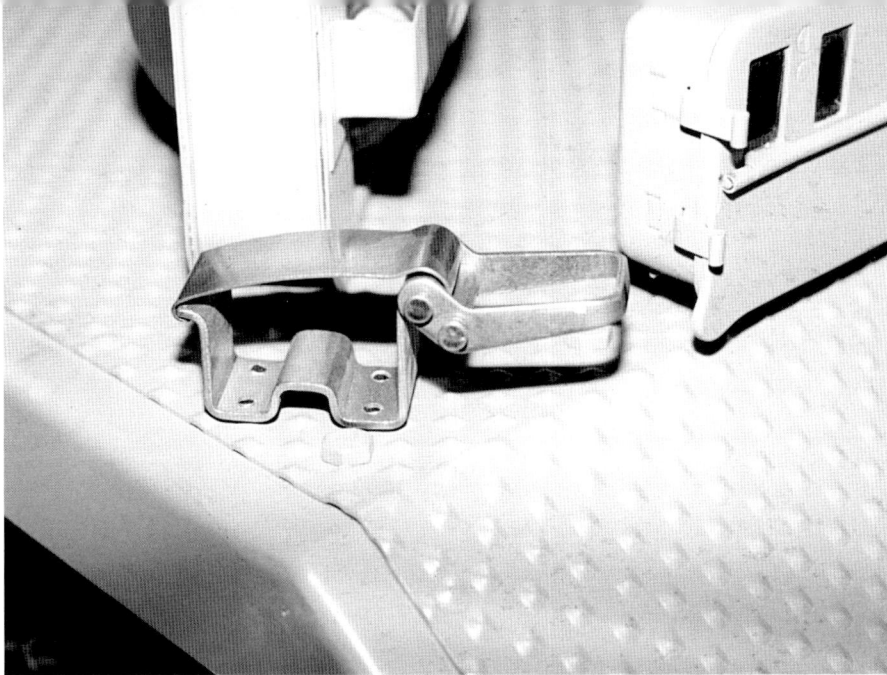

This reproduction clamp is one of the many types of tool clamp used on German military vehicles. Similar clamps also used a small wing nut to secure the hasp.

Late Fender Support

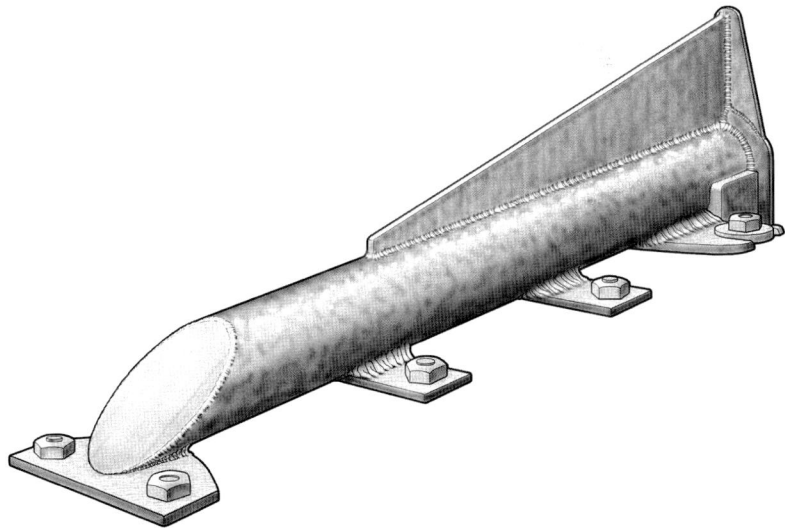

The early mudguard supports were simple tubes welded to the hull and bolted to the mud-guards. The support on this vehicle has been tack welded to the mudguard to keep it from falling apart. Later versions had a long reinforcing gusset welded to the top or were stamped metal shapes. This StuG III Ausf. G was originally equipped with smoke grenade launchers. The hole in the superstructure wall still has the launcher wiring leading into the fighting compartment.

StuG III Ausf. Gs were originally equipped with a box-shaped rear Notek light. The upper half was divided into four segments. At night, if the light appeared to be one light, then the following driver was too far behind. If the light appeared as four individual lights, then the distance was too close. Two lights indicated the correct distance.

The lower flap could be raised to reveal two red brake lights for daytime use. The small hole in the lower flap allowed the lower red light to shine through if the brakes were applied at night. Later vehicles were equipped with a blue tinted tubular distance light, although the earlier light remained in use to the end of the war.

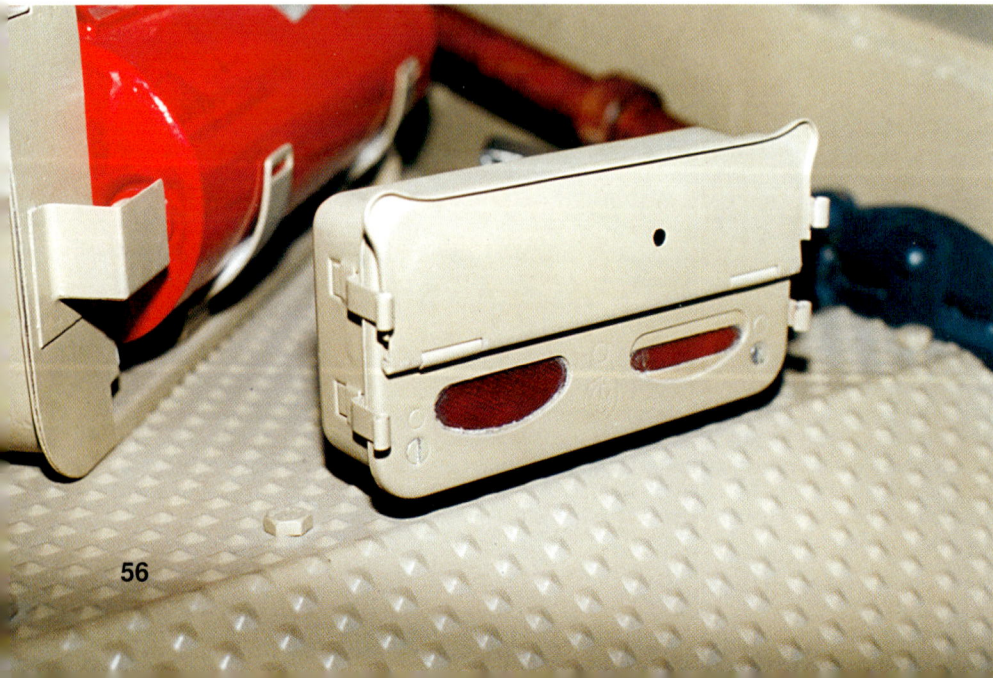

The gun barrel cleaning rods were heavy wooden dowels with threaded metal end connectors that could be joined together. The threaded ends were protected by a sheet metal box welded to the engine deck.

Tail Light (Mid/Late Production Vehicles)

The other ends of the gun barrel cleaning rods were held in place with a hinged bracket secured with a wing nut. The bore cleaning brush was protected by a small canvas bag that used a drawstring to keep it in place.

The StuG III Ausf. G incorporated a new commander's cupola, which provided all around vision for the vehicle commander. Originally, the cupola could be rotated through 360° on a ball bearing race. A shortage of ball bearings resulted in this feature being dropped in September of 1943. In August of 1944, the ball bearing race was again installed and saw use to the end of the war.

A spade was stowed on the left mudguard beside the engine intake. One end was held in place by a bent sheet metal strap shaped to the end of the spade, while the other end was secured with a clamp. The small bracket in the middle of the photograph is for the forward end of the pry bar, which is waiting to be installed on this restored StuG III Ausf. G.

Wire cutters were standard issue and used on most German armored vehicles. The end points guided the wire into the jaws.

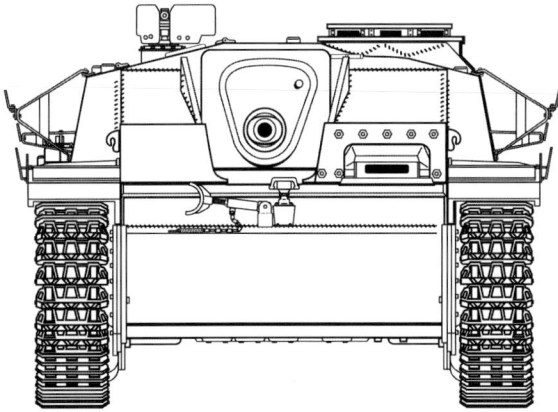

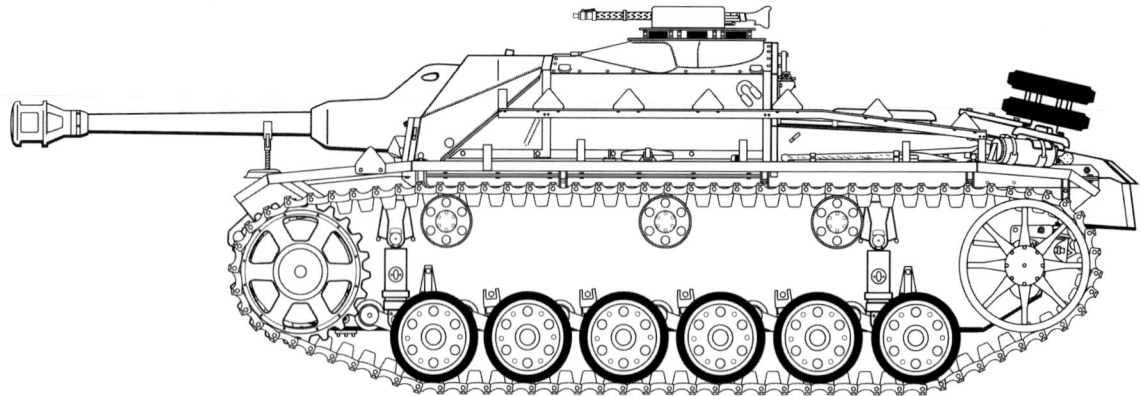

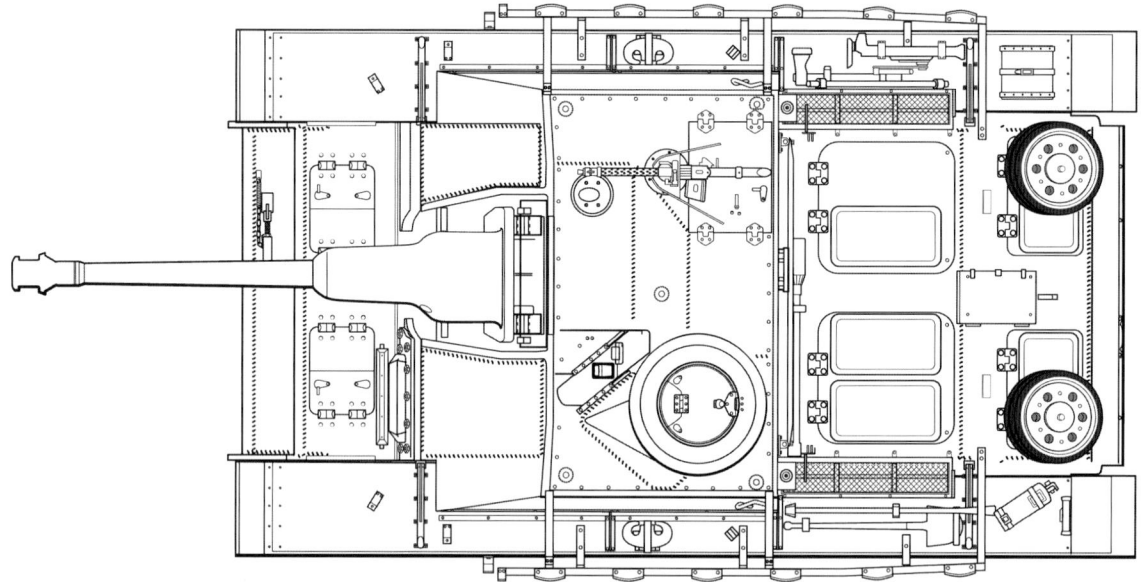

Sturmgeschütz III Ausf. G (Late) (Sd.Kfz 142/1) Specifications

Length:..................21.98 feet (6.7 M)

Width:...................9.68 feet (2.95 M)

Height:..................7.22 feet (2.2 M)

Empty Weight:......47,899 pounds (21,727 KG)

Loaded Weight:....57,098.8 pounds (25,900 KG)

Powerplant:..........One 265 HP Maybach HL 120 TRM V-12 12-cylinder, liquid-cooled engine

Transmission:......SSG 77 – Six speeds forward, one speed reverse

Armament:............One hull-mounted 7.5 CM StuK 40 gun with 54 rounds, one roof-mounted 7.92MM MG34 machine gun with 600 rounds, and one coaxial 7.92mm MG34 machine gun with 600 rounds

Maximum Speed:..24.86 MPH (40 KMH)

Range:..................96.3 miles (155 KM)

Crew:....................Four

A fairly late production StuG III Ausf. G crosses a river in France. The vehicle has 40 CM (15.75 inch) tracks with ice cleats, an 80MM (3.15 inch) front plate, the cupola shot deflector, and the cast *Topfblende* mantlet.

This Ausf. G is coated with *Zimmerit* and painted overall dark yellow. The rectangular port in the machine gun shield indicates the vehicle is equipped with the later 7.92MM MG42 machine gun.

A late production StuG III Ausf. G maneuvers along a tight street in a small French village during the summer of 1944. A layer of concrete has been applied to the top of the driver's compartment. The scalloped side skirts — top and bottom — are unusual, but not entirely unknown on late production PzKpfw III tanks and StuG III self-propelled guns.

British troops examine a late production Ausf. G abandoned by its crew on 27 August 1944. The vehicle has a *Topfblende* mantlet and late pattern track return rollers. Foliage camouflage was mandatory in order to hide German vehicles from roving Allied fighter-bombers — known as *Jabos* (*Jagdbomberen*) by the Germans.

(Above Left) Both the StuG III and PzKpfw III were equipped with a small metal toolbox containing a variety of screwdrivers and wrenches for basic vehicle maintenance. The tool kit was bolted to the center of the engine deck. The toolboxes differed slightly in the position of the lock hasp. Late versions had the hasp located in the center. Some hasps were protected by a hinged guard.

(Above) The interior of the metal toolbox was fitted with a wooden insert with sections routed out in the shape of each tool in the box.

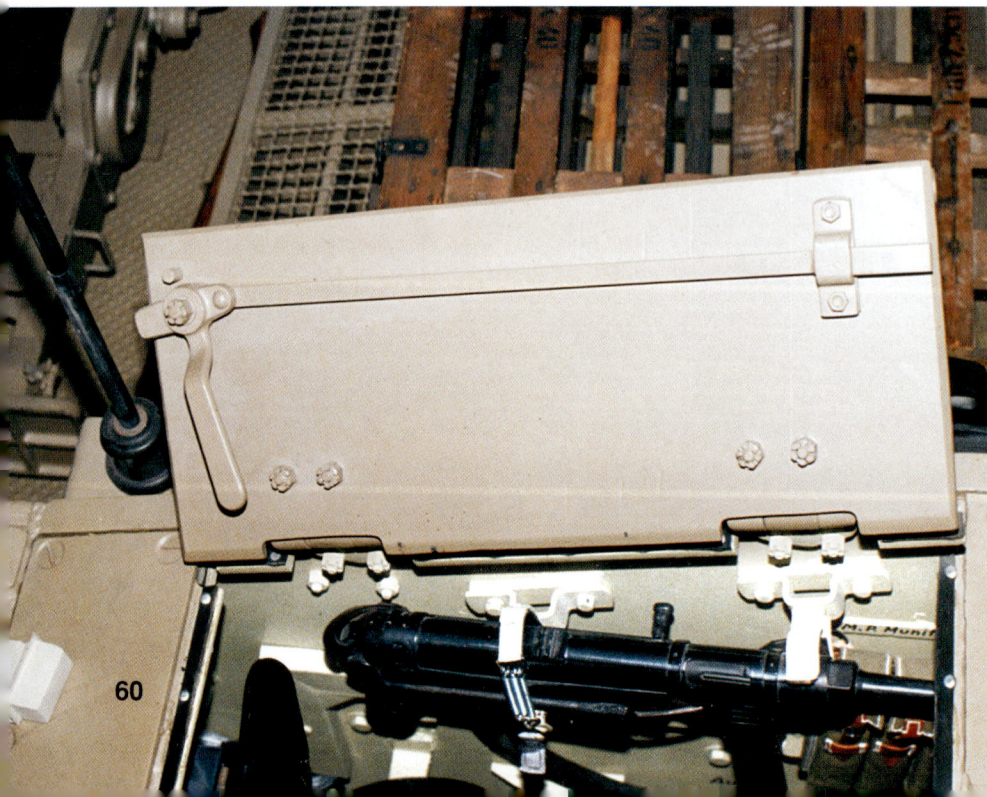

(Left) The rear loader's hatch was fitted with a locking bar that could be opened from the outside with a square key. The key was similar to the one used to open the glacis hatches.

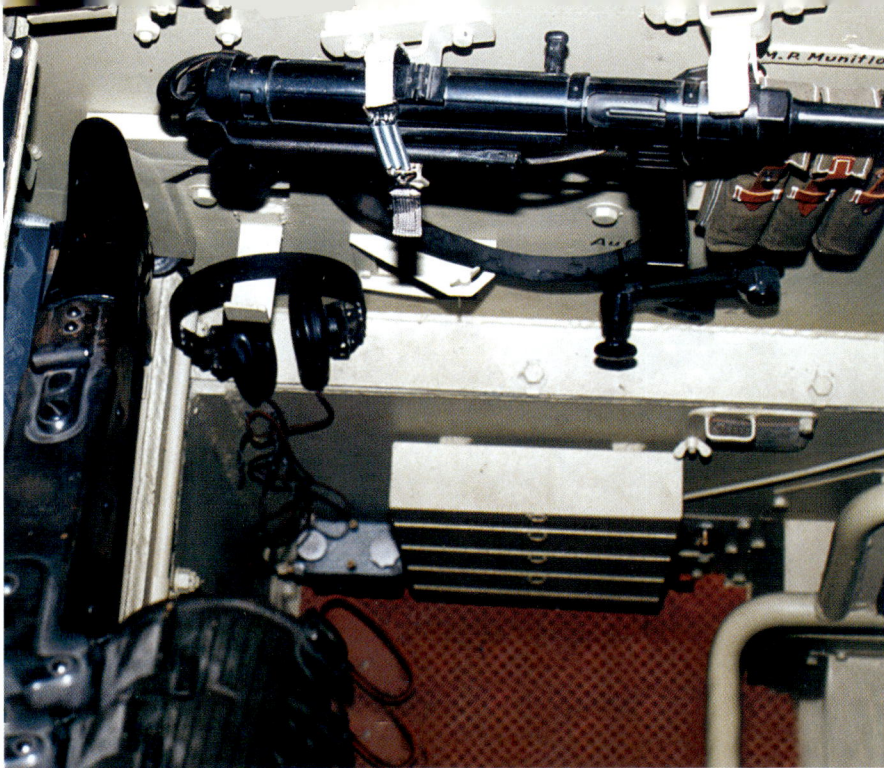

(Above) An MP40 sub-machine gun, known as a *Maschinenpistole* (literally, machine pistol) to the Germans, was stowed on the rear wall of the crew compartment. The canvas pouches contained three additional clips of 9mm ammunition.

(Above Right) A second MP40 was mounted on the left rear corner of the vehicle. The antenna cable leads from the antenna base, through a small hole in the rear armor plate, and on to the junction box mounted on the rear fighting compartment wall. The rack for the commander's FuG 15 USW receiver is mounted next to the junction box.

(Right) A small, swiveling metal cover located on the firewall between the engine and crew compartments provided access to the oil level gauge. The plate's U-shaped handle has been broken off, however its weld beads are still visible. The label has instructions relating to the size and arrangement of the roadwheel torsion bars.

The loader cradles a 7.5 CM *Panzergranate* (armor piercing) round prior to loading it into the gun breech. The rounds were fired electrically. The loader's MP40 is secured to the rear wall.

A sheet metal duct pulled fumes from above the gun breech and out through the fume extraction ventilator mounted on the rear wall of the crew compartment. It is painted with red oxide primer.

StuG III crews load 7.5 CM ammunition aboard their vehicle. Normal stowage amounted to some 54 armor-piercing and high explosive rounds stored in racks located around the fighting compartment.

The StuG Ausf. G was equipped with a 7.5 cm *Sturmkanone* (StuK) 40 L/48 gun. The weapon was similar to that used on the PzKpfw IV Ausf. G (late) through Ausf. J tanks, but had a revised recuperator assembly. Owing to space considerations, the StuG III recuperator was mounted on top of the gun rather than along the side. The weapon was inter- nally counterbalanced and equipped with double baffle muzzle brake to lessen both recoil forces and muzzle blast. Gun elevation ranged from -6 to +20° with 10° left and right tra- verse.

The SflZf1c direct fire gun sight was mounted on the left side of the gun breech. The embossed dial is the range indicator. An adjustable indicator was moved up or down on the range indicator to the selected dial. Elevation adjustment was made using the black twist handle on the bottom. A small light was mounted on the side of the breech guard to signal the gunner that the round was in place and the gun was ready to fire.

The gun employed a semi-automatic, falling block breech and was electrically fired from a trigger located on the hand traverse wheel. The breech automatically opened after firing and ejected the spent shell casing into a canvas bag suspended beneath the tubular breech guard. A vertical mount for another 9ᴍᴍ MP40 machine pistol is visible at right.

The right side of the breech of the 7.5 ᴄᴍ StuK 40 L/48 housed the round breech block opening mechanism. The small lever above it is the safety, which can be locked into the *Sicher* (safe) or *Feuer* (fire) positions.

A rack holding 15 rounds of 7.5 ᴄᴍ ammunition was located on the right side of the gun. A folding ready rack holding 15 more rounds was attached to the side of the hull closer to the loader. The ammunition rack is folded back against the side of the hull in this photograph. The plate with the stenciled words VERBANDS KASTEN (first-aid kit) is lying loose on the floor and does not belong there.

(Above) The fighting compartment roof was composed of several welded plates ranging from 11MM to 17MM thick. The outer edges were angled down to meet the side panniers. A hole was cut into the armor above the gunner's head to provide an aperture for the SflZf1c direct fire gun sight. The box below the opening held flares for the flare pistol. The black bracket at lower left held an intercom speaker. The chassis, or *'Fahrgestell'* number, painted inside the roof indicates the vehicle was manufactured at the MIAG plant.

(Above Right) The *Nahverteidigungswaffe* (close-in defense weapon) was mounted on new StuG III Ausf. G beginning in May of 1944. Some vehicles had the weapon's port plated over, since the *Nahverteidigungswaffe* was only available in limited numbers. The weapon fired a variety of ammunition and signal flares and could be loaded and fired from within the vehicle.

(Right) The driver was confined to a narrow compartment in front of the gunner. The driver's seat folded down for access. Both steering levers are visible just in front of the seat. The StuG III's turning radius amounted to some 5.85 M (19.2 feet).

The missing roof plate on this damaged and abandoned StuG III Ausf. G reveals the 7.5 cm gun's recuperator housing and the ammunition stowage racks on the right side of the fighting compartment. The 15 round rack is mounted on the lower hull, while an eight round rack is located in the front sponson. The loader's ready rack has been unfolded at the bottom. The circumstances surrounding this vehicle are unclear; the left side of the fighting compartment appears to have suffered fire damage, while the right side is fairly well intact. The gun is in full recoil.

The gunner worked in close proximity to the gun and gunsight. The gun's breechblock is in the foreground. The StuG III's interior was painted a pale cream color to improve lighting.

Dummy rounds are stowed in the folding ready ammunition rack immediately in front of the loader. Empty racks could be folded against the hull side when not needed. This provided more working space to the loader and gave access to the ammunition bins in the front of the compartment. Due to a short supply of brass, Germany made extensive use of shellacked steel cartridge casings during the war.

A technician works on the StuG III's front drive units within the narrow confines of the driver's compartment. The vehicle's driver was generally responsible for the automotive maintenance, while specialist units accomplished heavy maintenance.

The driver sat inside a narrow armored box. The *Fahrersehklappe* 50 driver's visor was mounted directly in front and set into the 50mm (1.97 inch) armor plate. The bolts on the inside secured an additional 30mm (1.18 inch) armor plate to the outside. This arrangement remained in use throughout the StuG III Ausf. G's production.

The mounting racks for the FuG 16 10 watt transmitter and USW receiver were set into the right pannier where they were easily accessed by the loader/radio operator. Below the rightmost rack is a ground plate for the dynamotor, which provided the 12-volt radio power supply.

The Sf14Z *Scherenfernrohr* scissors periscope was mounted on the angled pipe hanging down from the commander's cupola. The periscopes are all missing from the cupola. An MP40 machine gun bracket is secured to the rear wall of the fighting compartment at left, while the FuG 15 USW radio receiver rack is set into the left pannier.

A rack holding eight more 7.5 cm rounds was fitted into this space above the lower rack. The total ammunition load amounted to 54 rounds, however this was often exceeded in practice. The bracket for the MP40 machine pistol and *Nahverteidigungswaffe* are also visible.

A ground plate for the dynamotor was also attached to the left side of the crew compartment immediately in front of the FuG 15 USW radio mount. The box with the partly open lid is believed to have been used to store the headset. The empty mount for the vehicle intercom speaker is directly above the box.

Two large handles were used to move the driver's armored visor into one of four positions. Two adjustable pins engaged the notches in the outer frame to hold the visor in position. The two small levers at the top of the visor held a block of armored glass in place behind the rectangular hinged frame. A rubber padded forehead rest was provided at the top to allow the driver to get as close as possible to the glass for the best possible view.

The StuG III was steered using two levers. The accelerator and clutch pedals were mounted on the floor. The left final drive unit runs above the pedals. The driver's pistol port plug is directly to the left of the front visor. The plug was held in place by a locking bar and secured by a large wing nut, which fit over a recess machined around the base of the plug. The plug retaining chain is also visible.

The commander and gunner sat in close proximity to each other and more-or-less in line with the driver. The commander's Sf14Z *Scherenfernrohr* scissors periscope is directly in front of his face.

The Sf14Z *Scherenfernrohr* periscope provided a binocular view of the surrounding area. The periscope was mounted to the cupola race and could be rotated through 360°. The Sfl4Z could also be dismounted and used outside the vehicle.

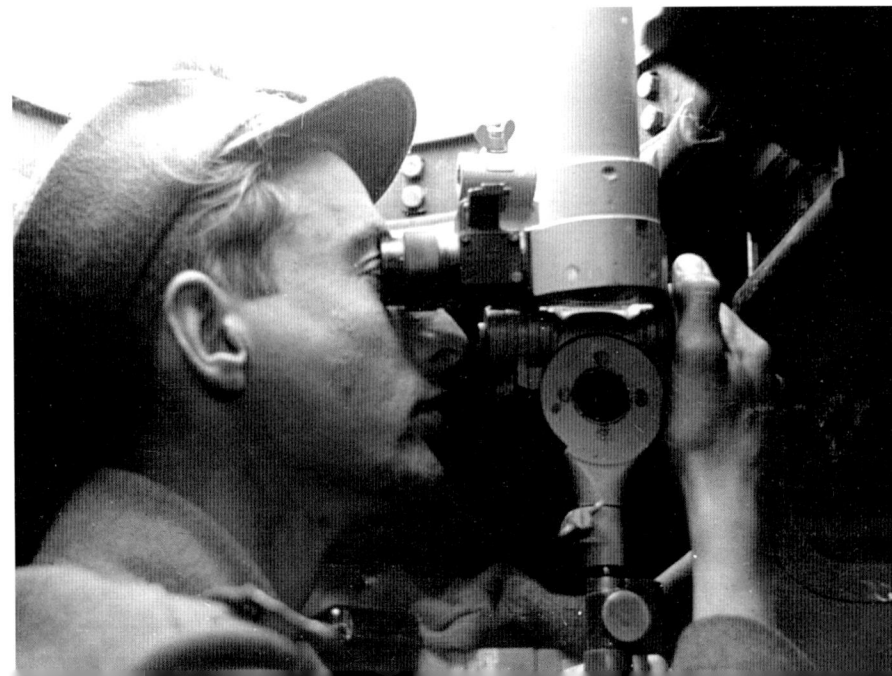

A rack holding 15 rounds of 7.5 cm ammunition was mounted in the lower right portion of the fighting compartment. An eight round rack was normally set into the space above the 15 round rack. The racks were basically sheet metal and provided no protection for the rounds inside.

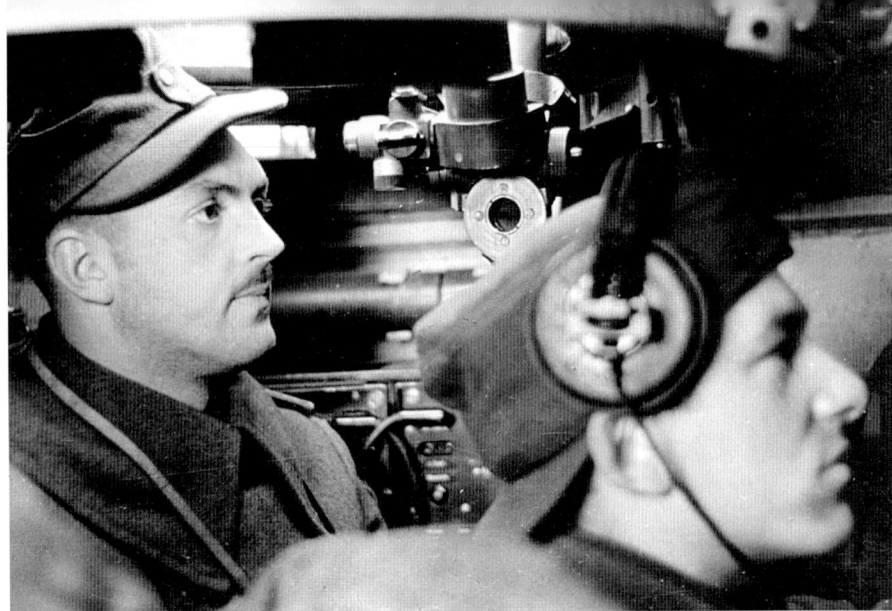

StuG III Ausf. Gs, believed to be later production vehicles with the welded mantlet, move along a muddy Russian road. Mud from the tracks is being thrown up on the mudguards and vehicle stowage. The trailing vehicle has an additional set of half panels mounted over the center *Schürzen*.

This StuG III Ausf. G on display represents the final production model. It is equipped with the late pattern track return rollers, 80мм (3.15 inch) hull and fighting compartment armor

German troops clamber aboard a StuG III Ausf. G in Russia during the winter of 1943/1944. This vehicle is equipped with smaller skirts held in place with diamond shaped retainers. A second set of armored shields are angled against the upper side of the fighting compartment. Buried under the mass of soldiers are at least two Russian heavy machine guns on wheeled carriages.

plates, the remote controlled machine gun mount, and the late cast mantlet. Although not visible, this mantlet does have the MG port drilled into the upper left corner.

Spare track links were often used as a form of additional armor protection. This late production StuG III Ausf. G is fitted with 80mm (3.15 inch) hull and fighting compartment armor, a remote control machine gun mount on the roof of the crew compartment, *Pilze* mounts for the 2-ton jib crane, and steel return rollers.

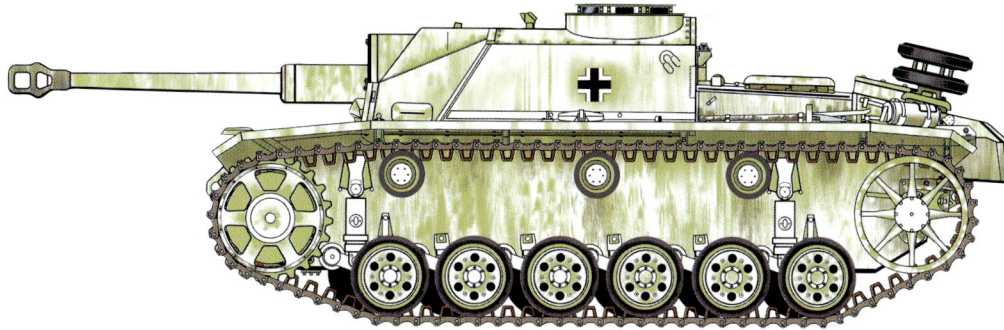

This early StuG III Ausf. G from StuG *Abteilung* (Battalion) 226 operated in the Lake Ladoga area of Russia during the winter of 1942-43. Produced in December of 1942, the front plate of the pannier over the mudguard is steeply sloped and the drivers side visor has been retained from the previous production vehicles.

Florian Geyer, another early production StuG III Ausf. G, was assigned to SS-StuG Abt 2, 2.SS-Panzer-Grenadier-Division *'Das Reich,'* in Russia during the summer of 1943. The driver's side visor was replaced on this vehicle by a pistol port plug. Spare track links are wrapped around the spare wheels mounted atop the engine deck.

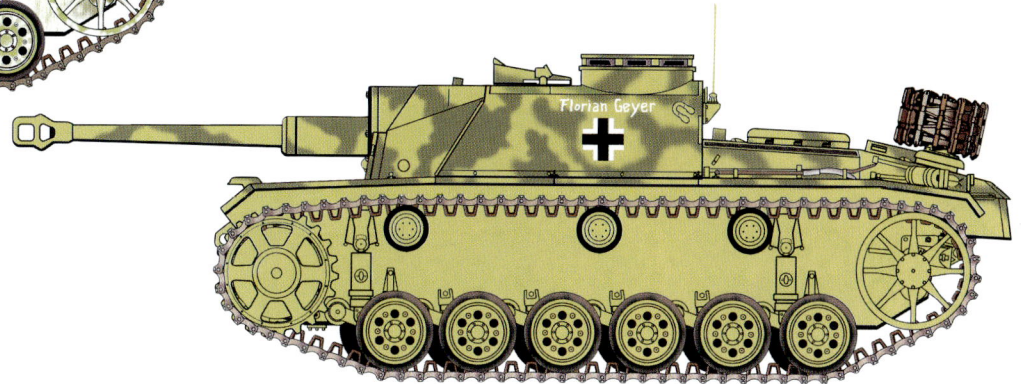

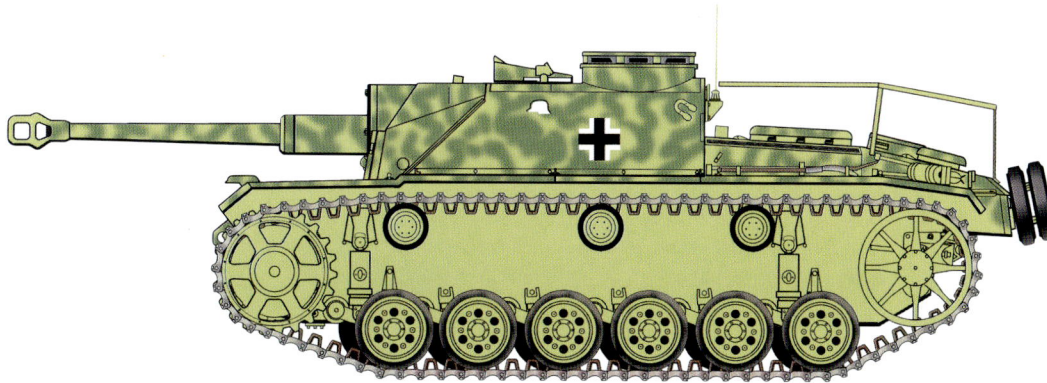

This early StuG III Ausf. G served with StuG Abt *'Großdeutschland'* near Akhtyrka, Russia in May of 1943. It is one of several built in January of that year on the hulls of PzKpfw III and featured one piece hatches on the glacis. It still retains the hinged rear flap while the front one is now fixed, although hinged front flaps were also seen. The *Großdeutschland's* white helmet insignia is painted on the upper hull sides.

Another early StuG III Ausf. G built on a PzKpfw III chassis was this vehicle from Panzer-Grenadier-Division *'Feldherrnhalle'* in St. Raphael, France during the summer of 1943. It also has one piece glacis hatches and is equipped with the deep wading exhaust introduced on the PzKpfw III Ausf. M, along with hinged front and rear mudguards.

The StuG III Ausf. G jack was normally stowed on the right rear mudguard. The brackets and jack on this restored StuG III are not original equipment, although they closely resemble the originals.

Restored vehicles or museum examples are often fitted with modern replicas of tools and equipment such as this axe and the mesh screen protecting the engine air intake. This makes it difficult for the uninitiated enthusiast to determine what is authentic and what is not. The original mesh screen was woven and had a diamond shape.

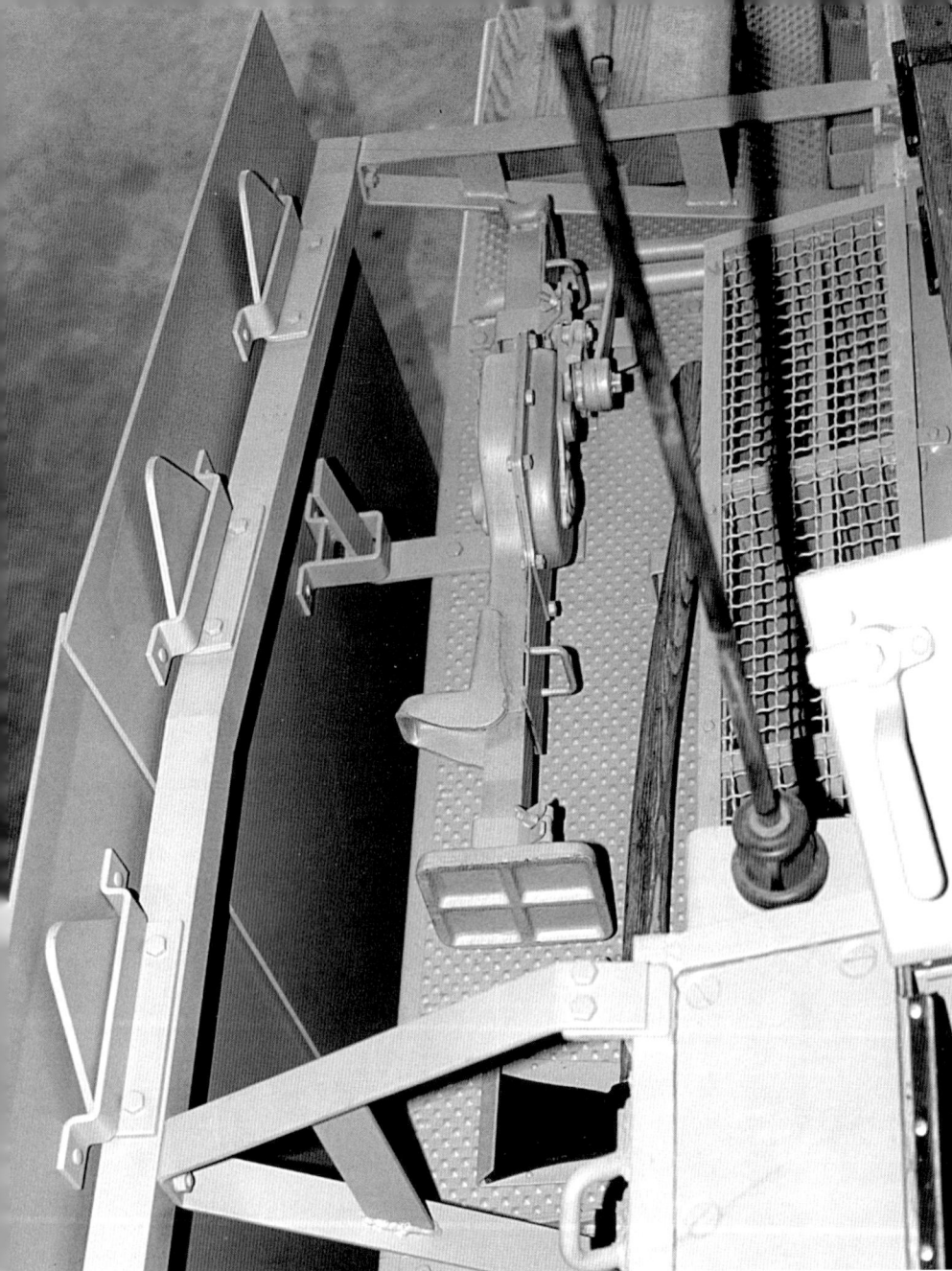

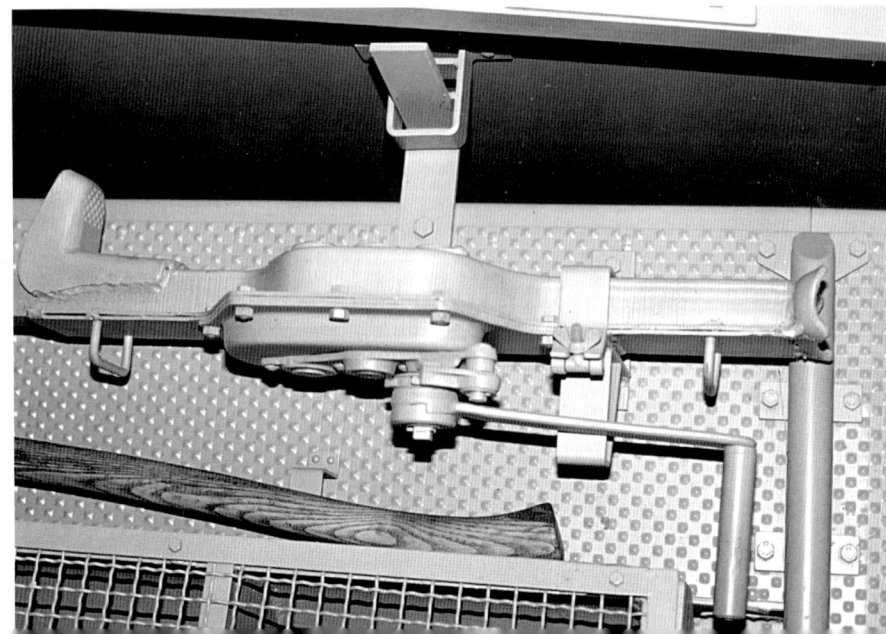

The jack, axe, and jack block are stowed on the right mudguard. The side skirts were approximately 5MM thick and hung from saw-toothed flanges bolted to the angle rail. A second set of brackets allowed the lower ends of the skirts to be adjusted outward to clear the wider *Ostketten* or *Winterketten* tracks.

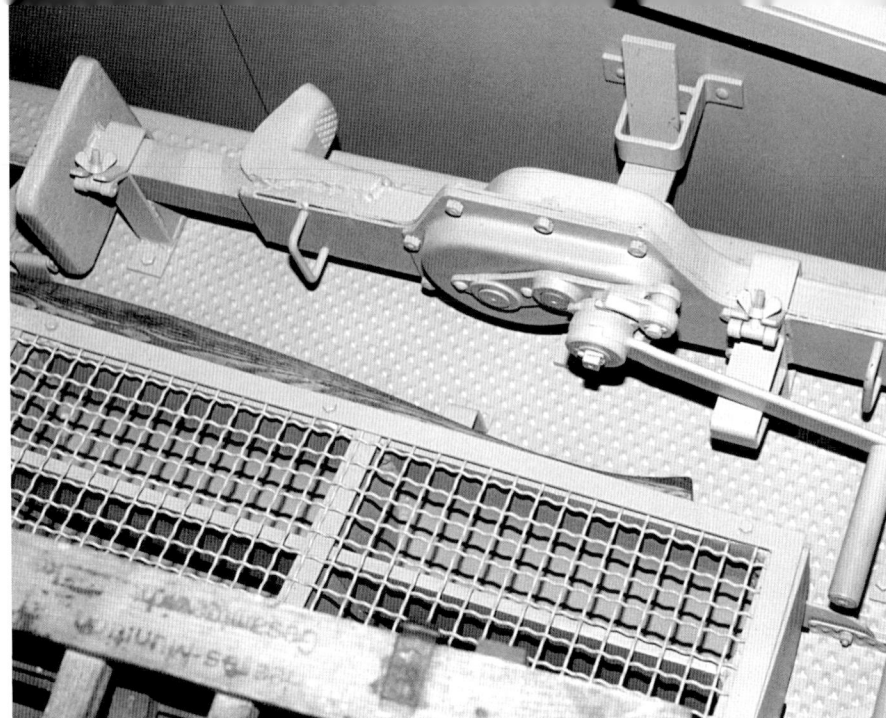

(Above) Winter camouflaged Panzer Grenadiers pose around a late production StuG III Ausf. G during the late winter of 1944. The vehicle has been given a scruffy coat of winter whitewash. Six black kill rings are painted around the end of the gun barrel.

(Above Right) This *Zimmerit* coated and well camouflaged late production Ausf. G was assigned to a *Fallschirmjäger* (Airborne) unit during the summer of 1944. Two C-hooks are dangling from the front tow eyes.

(Right) Five StuG III Ausf. Gs are garaged in France in early 1944. The vehicles have late production hulls, middle production fighting compartments, cast mantlets, and machine gun shields designed for use with the MG42. The vehicles are coated with *Zimmerit* and all wear a coat of dark yellow camouflage paint.

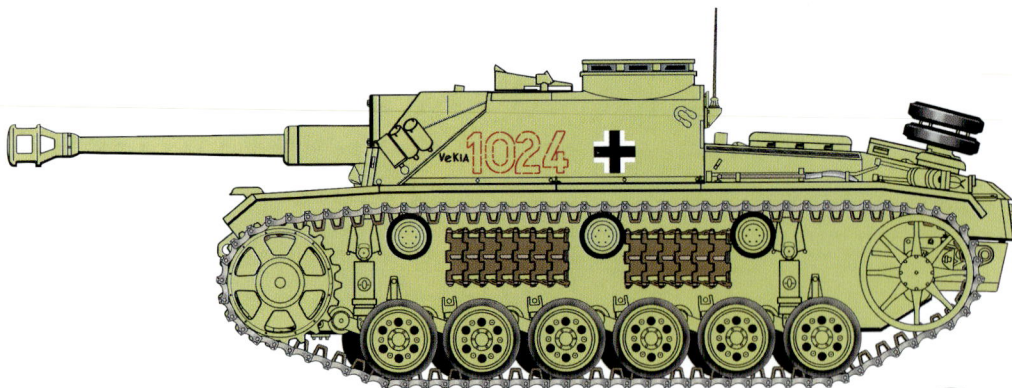

This mid-production StuG III Ausf. G (1024) is assigned to III./Pz.Rgt.2, 16.Panzer-Division in Rome, Italy, during November of 1943. From February to May of 1943, smoke grenade launchers were installed on each side of the superstructure. The launchers were fired electrically from inside the vehicle. The crew have attached additional track links to the lower hull sides for additional protection.

A mid-production StuG III Ausf. G during Operation CITADEL in July of 1943. Side skirt armor (*Schürzen*), for protection against anti-tank rifles, began to be fitted to new vehicles in April and May of 1943 in time for the Kursk offensive. They were easily lost during combat and the rear plate has been replaced with one painted in a different camouflage paint scheme.

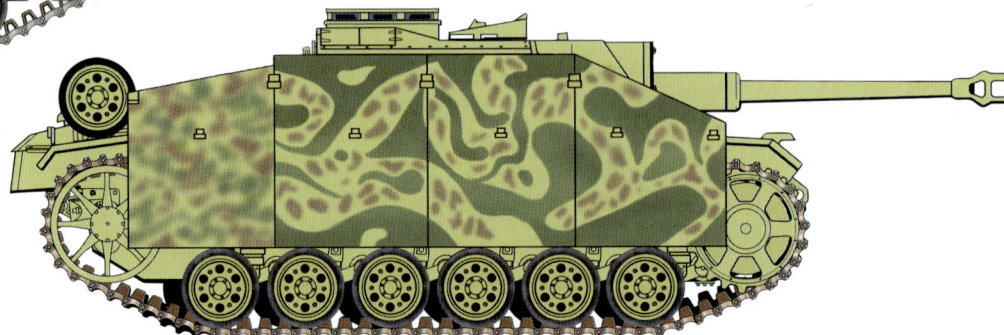

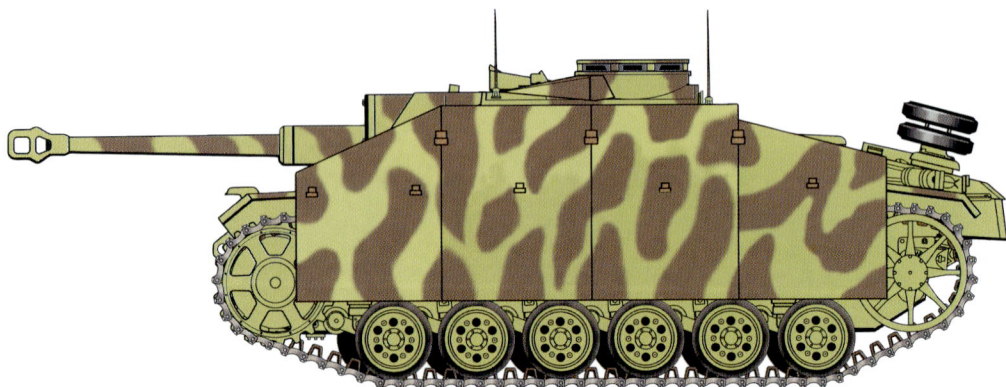

This mid-production StuG III Ausf. G was assigned to Pz.Kp. (FKL) (Radio-Controlled Tank Company) 316 in Grafenwohr, Germany in September of 1943. The unit's vehicles were fitted with an additional antenna on the left front of the superstructure roof – used for the radio equipment controlling their Borgward B IV remote control demolition vehicles.

Another mid-production StuG III Ausf. G served in Russia in late 1943 or early 1944. Two additional plates were added to the *Schürzen* beside the crew compartment, which provided a measure of extra protection. The front plate was also replaced.

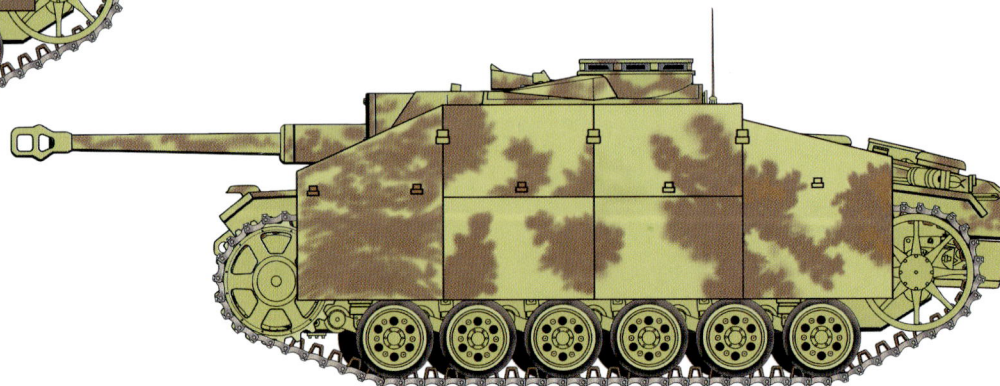

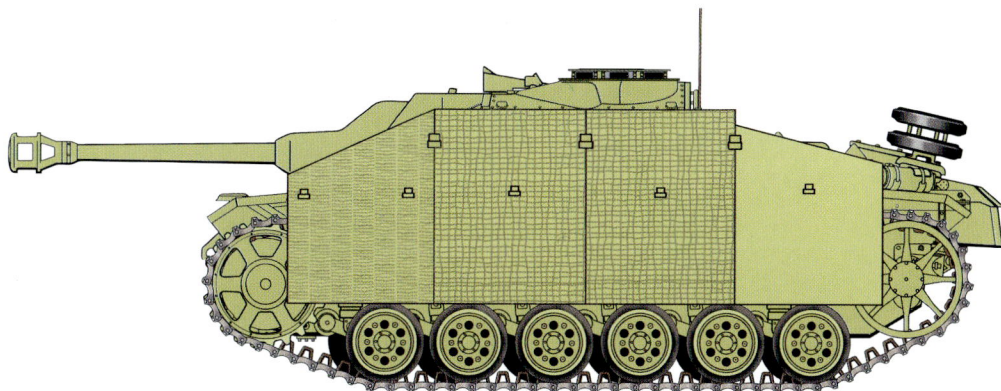

This late production StuG III Ausf. G, seen in Russia during the spring of 1944, is equipped with the new cast gun mantlet or *Topfblende* (pot mantlet). It was introduced on some vehicles beginning in November of 1943. Additionally, the StuG III is fitted with *Schürzen* and the *Zimmerit* anti-magnetic mine coating on the hull introduced in September of 1943. Unusually, *Zimmerit* has also been applied on some of the *Schürzen*.

This late production StuH 42 Ausf. G (131) was deployed to Russia during the summer of 1944. It is equipped with the *Topfblende* cast gun mantlet, a shot deflector in front of the cupola, and the waffle pattern *Zimmerit* coating. The *Schürzen* have been modified so that the bottom sections will pivot on their supports, thereby preventing them from being snagged and torn off by brush. This became a fairly common practice in many *Sturmgeschütz* units. A red tactical sign for a self-propelled artillery battalion is painted on the upper *Schürzen*.

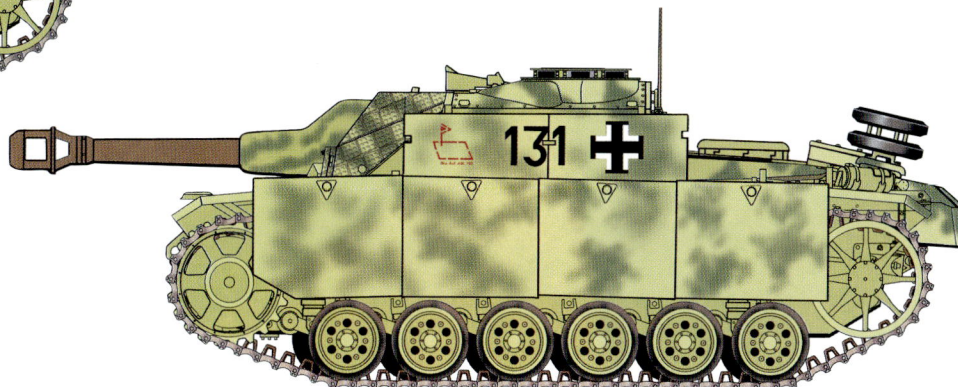

This late production StuG III Ausf. G (111) saw service in Russia during the late fall of 1944. The crew has painted the eyes, ears, and tusks of an elephant's head on the *Topfblende* cast gun mantlet. *Zimmerit* was no longer applied to StuG IIIs beginning in September of 1944.

A late production StuG. III Ausf. G in Germany in the spring of 1945, with all the final modifications. These include a *Topfblende* cast gun mantlet with coaxial machine gun, remote control machine gun mount on the roof of the fighting compartment, cast steel return rollers, and final pattern *Schürzen* brackets.

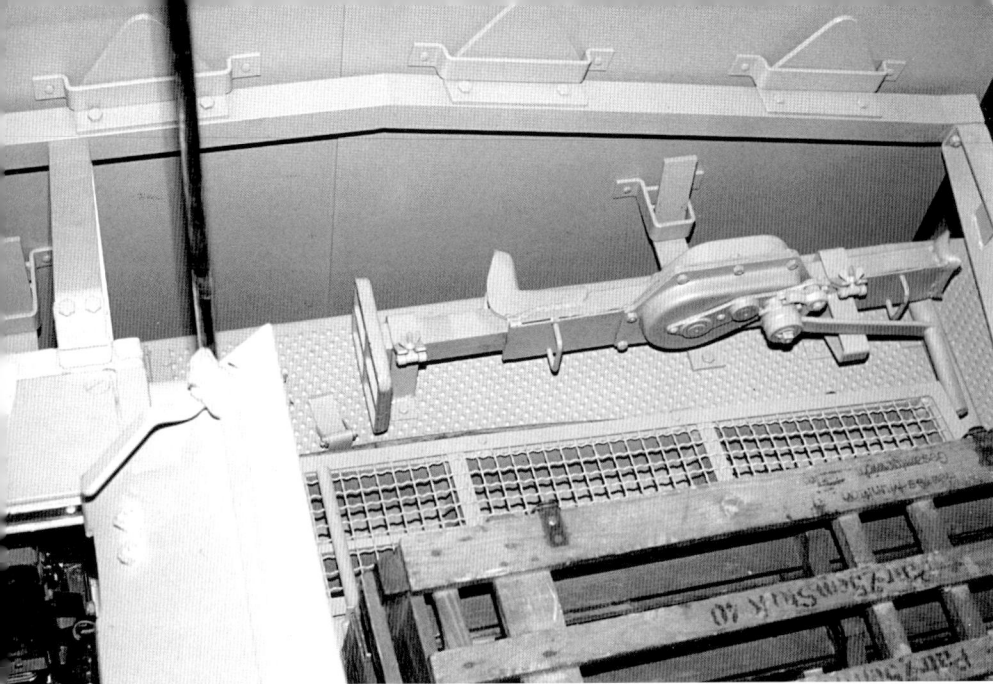

The *Patr* 7.5 *cm* KwK 40 and StuK 40 ammunition was shipped in simple wooden crates. Each crate held three rounds of ammunition. The StuK 40 fired three types of ammunition, the *Sprenggranat-Patrone* 34 high explosive round, the *Panzergranat-Patrone* 39 armor piercing round, and the less common *Panzergranat-Patrone* 40 tungsten core armor piercing round.

The ammunition crates were of sturdy wooden construction with dovetailed joints, hinged on one side and fitted with two clasps on the other so they could be recovered and reused. Scalloped rests inside the crate prevented the rounds from rolling around.

Middle production StuG III Ausf. Gs roll past dug-in German troops on the steppes of the eastern front during the late spring of 1944. Both vehicles are coated with *Zimmerit* and are equipped with cast *Topfblende* mantlets. Additional track links are being used to improve protection across the front of the vehicle.

StuG III Ausf. Gs assembled at the Alkett plant between December of 1943 and September of 1944 were coated with their unique waffle pattern *Zimmerit*. The idea was to prevent the enemy — most notably the Russians — from planting magnetic explosives against the hull. *Zimmerit* was used on most tanks and self-propelled guns and was applied to all vertical to nearly horizontal armor plate that was conceivably within reach of a man standing on the ground. *Zimmerit* also found its way onto some sheet metal surfaces as well. Its use was discontinued when it was realized there was little or no threat from hand placed magnetic explosives.

The StuG III Ausf. G was also built as a self-propelled howitzer mounting a 10.5 CM howitzer, designated the *Sturmhaubitze* (StuH) 42. Production of the StuH 42 Ausf. G began in March of 1943. The vehicle was used on all fronts in the infantry support role.

The StuH 42 chassis and hull went through the same course of improvements made to the StuG Ausf. G. Black 55 still has the bulged fan belt inspection cover on the hull rear and some of the earlier stowage arrangements on the rear mudguards. The vehicle is equipped with the later tubular style taillight on the left rear mudguard.

The only real difference between the StuG III Ausf. G and the StuH 42 Ausf. G was the gun, the gun mount, and the internal ammunition storage. The vehicle employed a variant of the 10.5 CM IFH18 howitzer used by the Wespe self-propelled artillery mount — itself a variant of the basic towed artillery piece used by the German Army. Only 36 of the larger 10.5 CM rounds could be carried internally with some of these rounds being special shaped charge rounds for use against armor should the need arise.

Middle production StuH 42s cross a muddy valley in Rumania during the spring of 1943. Owing to the reasonably clean features, full skirts, and muzzle covers, the vehicles are believed to be on a training exercise. Final production StuH 42s were equipped with the roof mounted remote controlled machine gun and often lacked a muzzle brake.

Smoke, Steel, and the Roar of the Gun.
More World War Two Armor

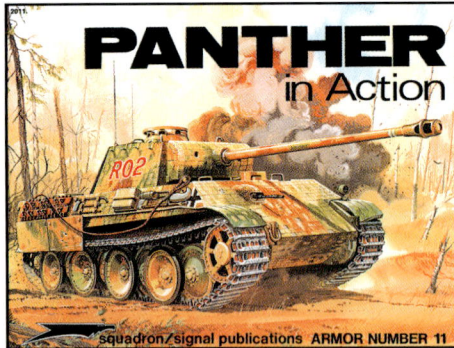

2011 Panther

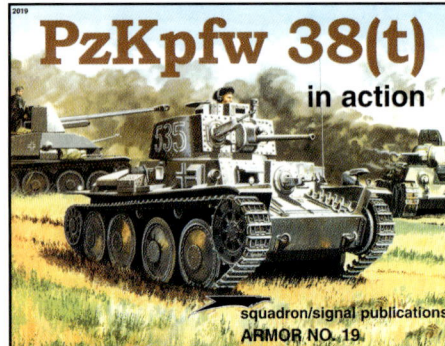

2019 PzKpfw 38(t)

2020 T-34

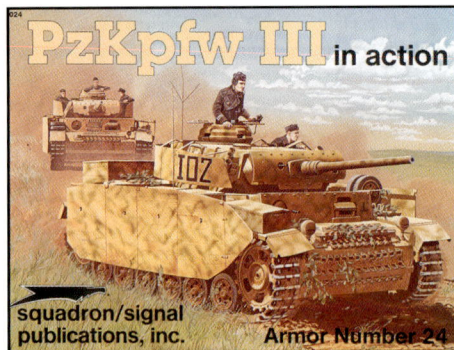

2024 PzKpfw III

2027 Tiger

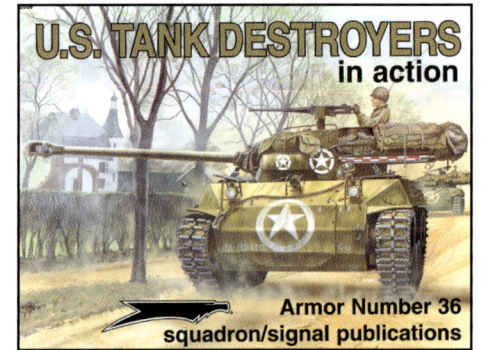

2036 US Tank Destroyers

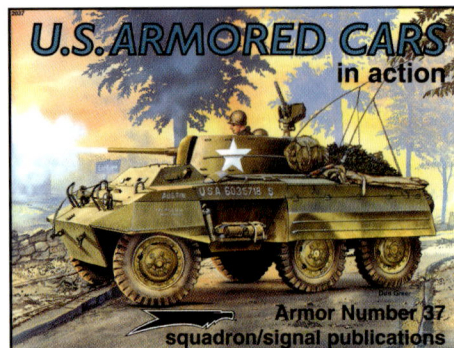

2037 US Armored Cars

2039 Italian Medium Tanks

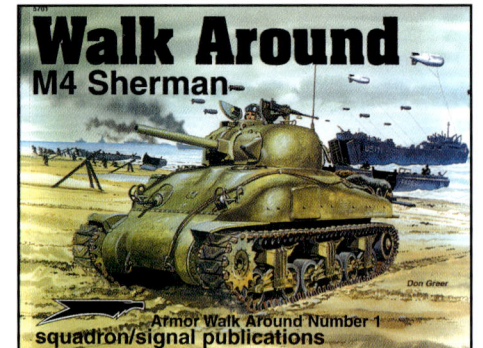

5701 M4 Sherman

From squadron/signal publications